How to Pass
the UK's National
Firefighter
Selection Process

How to Pass
the UK's National Firefighter Selection Process

Everything you need to know to succeed in the national assessments

3rd edition

Mike Bryon

KoganPage

LONDON PHILADELPHIA NEW DELHI

First published in Great Britain in 2004 as *How to Pass the Firefighter Selection Process* by Kogan Page Limited
Reprinted 2005, 2008
Second edition 2008
Third edition 2011

2nd Floor
45 Gee Street
London EC1V 3RS
United Kingdom

© Mike Bryon, 2004, 2008, 2011

ISBN   978 0 7494 6205 5
E-ISBN   978 0 7494 6206 2

British Library Cataloguing-in-Publication Data

A CIP record for this book is available from the British Library.

Library of Congress Cataloging-in-Publication Data

Bryon, Mike.
    How to pass the UK's national firefighter selection process : everything you need to succeed in the national assessments / Mike Bryon. – 3rd ed.
        p. cm.
    Originally published: How to pass the firefighter selection process. 1st ed. London : Kogan Page, 2004.
    Includes bibliographical references.
    ISBN 978-0-7494-6205-5 – ISBN 978-0-7494-6206-2   1. Fire extinction–Great Britain–Examinations–Study guides.   2. Fire extinction–Great Britain–Examinations, questions, etc.
I. Bryon, Mike. How to pass the firefighter selection process.   II. Title.
    TH9157.B79 2011
    628.9'25076–dc22   2011000676

Typeset by Graphicraft Ltd, Hong Kong
Printed and bound by CPI Group (UK) Ltd, Croydon, CR0 4YY

Contents

Acknowledgements

'Fantastic. With the guidance from this book I have been able to progress to the interview stage with North Wales Fire and Rescue Service.'

Reader review

Use this book to find your way successfully through the UK's national firefighter selection process. Over 10,000 copies have been sold and it has become almost required reading for applicant firefighters. You most certainly can improve your score in the assessments that make up the firefighter selection process. Hard work, determination and, most of all, systematic preparation can lead to a significant improvement in your performance. For hundreds of candidates the exercises and advice contained in this book have meant the difference between pass and fail.

The content evolved from a series of applicant firefighter courses on which I taught, and I owe thanks to the candidates who attended those courses. They showed such incredible commitment and determination to succeed in their desire to become firefighters. If any failed a stage of the recruitment process then I was always impressed that they found the strength of character to apply again. Most of them are now serving firefighters and I wish them every success in their chosen career. I also owe thanks to the many hundreds of applicant firefighters who have e-mailed me seeking advice and sources of further practice material. Their queries have ensured that this title remains contemporary.

The practice questions in this book are intended only as a means to prepare for the real tests and interview, and the information contained should not be used for any other purpose. If a passage is on the subject of fire or fire safety, then please remember that it has been written for the purposes of preparing for the firefighter recruitment process only and under no circumstances should it be relied on as a source of advice on how to prevent or fight fire.

The views expressed are not those of any of the fire authorities or any serving firefighter or officer but are drawn from my experience of helping applicant firefighters through the recruitment process.

I am indebted to Philip Wilson, who undertook a read of the second edition of this title, suggested a series of improvements and corrected a number of errors. Any remaining errors or omissions are entirely mine.

This 3rd edition includes an expanded section on the situational awareness paper and information on spatial recognition, fault diagnosis and visual estimation assessments.

May I take this opportunity to wish you every success in fulfilling your ambition of becoming a firefighter.

CHAPTER 1

A career as a firefighter

The indispensable guide for applicant firefighters

If you are one of the many people whose ambition it is to become a firefighter, then this book can make it a reality. The previous editions have already helped thousands of candidates. This new edition can help you.

Most successful candidates spend a considerable amount of time and effort preparing for each stage of the firefighter recruitment process. Passing might well involve one of the biggest commitments you have made in your life so far. If this sounds a bit of an exaggeration, then appreciate that you will be one of many really determined candidates and some of them will have spent hours each week for months preparing. Do the same or risk coming a poor second.

Read this book carefully, think over the advice – discuss points with someone, complete the exercises even if you find them boring or difficult, and refer back to the relevant section as you progress through each stage of the real recruitment process. You are going to have to take a careful look at yourself. You may well have to work hard in order to master things that you have previously struggled with. Most applicants do. You may excel in some aspects of the firefighter selection process but, like many other people, will find one or more elements a real challenge. To succeed you are going to have to overcome these challenges and take full advantage of your strengths. You are going to have to present yourself as an applicant who would make a really good firefighter. If you do not follow this advice then you may well experience failure and have to find the strength of character to re-apply. It is not uncommon for applicants to fail five or more times before being accepted into the Fire Service.

The national standards

All the UK fire authorities put applicants through the same long and difficult recruitment process governed by national standards. It can easily last over six months. It assesses all candidates in terms of qualities such as their personality, community awareness, numerical and verbal skills, and physical fitness. Only applicants possessing the qualities that a firefighter needs will succeed. This book will guide you through each stage, helping you to present yourself as the ideal candidate.

If you have applied and failed before

If you have been through the process before, perhaps more than once, you might feel resentful and view it as unfair. Put any feelings of resentment and frustration aside, as they are counterproductive. The best frame of mind to adopt is one where you view the recruitment process as an opportunity. See it as your chance to prove that you have what it takes to be a firefighter. Better still, view the recruitment process as a long line of opportunities. Set about leaving no room for doubt and make sure that at every point in that long line you look and sound like a great candidate.

The role of the firefighter and key responsibilities

Working in pressurized situations

Part of the work of a firefighter is necessarily reactive. The general public expects our Fire Service to be at the ready, respond at speed to an emergency and deal with that emergency professionally.

It is common to think of firefighters as heroes who save the lives of people in danger from fire, road accidents or flood. Accounts of their bravery are regularly reported in our newspapers and a great many people are extremely grateful for the life-saving help they have provided.

The drama and action of an emergency is a major reason why so many people want to become firefighters. Physically firefighters need to be very fit, and to succeed in your application you will need to demonstrate a high degree of physical fitness.

Working as part of a team to resolve an emergency

Dealing with emergencies requires firefighters to work closely together, and you will have to prove that you too can work effectively as part of a team.

To fight a fire or rescue someone trapped in a lift or a crashed car requires teamwork of the highest order. You are bound to be questioned about your understanding of what makes a good team and when you have been an effective member of a successful team.

What is teamwork?

Teamwork is the ability to work together towards a common goal. Good teamwork depends on effective communication, an equal contribution by each member of the team and a 'support one another' mentality. When a team is working at its best, it is amazing what it can accomplish and it is very likely that the objective will be realized.

How can you demonstrate that you have been an effective member of a team?

It is extremely likely that you have worked as a team to achieve something, solve a problem or sort out something unexpected. It may have been when you were at school or work, through voluntary work, through your involvement in a religious organization or a sports team. It is equally likely that you have played an effective role in a successful team. The objective of the team could be almost anything: win a game, paint a church hall or complete the day's work. It does not really matter what sort of team it was or what its objective was. All that matters is that you can describe how you were an effective member of a team and that it realized its objective. I have already explained that teamwork relies on good communication, an equal contribution of effort and mutual support, and this is irrespective of the common objective. Write down three or four examples of times when you worked as part of an effective team, what your common objective was and how its success was made possible through communication, equal effort and mutual support. Ask someone to question you about teamwork and be sure that you can confidently describe the occasions when you were part of a winning team and what made it so.

Working in hot, dirty confined spaces and at heights

Firefighters must work and operate equipment in dirty, wet, hot conditions, at heights, and sometimes in conditions where visibility is greatly restricted. You may be asked to describe occasions when you have coped in such circumstances, and you will have to take assessments that test your ability to complete a task under such conditions.

Dealing sympathetically with people who are emotional and distressed

Firefighters witness distressing situations and sometimes have to comfort and assist people who are extremely distressed. You should identify a time when you have dealt with such a situation or assisted people in such a state, and be sure that you can talk about that situation confidently.

Helping challenging members of the community

Not everyone is grateful for the service provided by the Fire Service. People who are intoxicated, for example, are far more likely to require the services of a firefighter but may not always welcome that help. They may on occasion react aggressively when assisted. Some people may appear undeserving. Yet firefighters must help every member of the public in the same way, no matter what they might think of them or how challenging they may be. Be prepared to describe any experience you have had of working with such members of the public, and expect to be questioned about your approach towards them.

Demonstrating integrity

Firefighters often find themselves in positions of great trust, entering people's homes and businesses after the occupier has left, assisting the elderly and children, and collecting abandoned possessions. There must be no question about their honesty or integrity. Expect to answer questions about your sincerity and truthfulness.

Working unsocial hours

Shift working and time spent on standby form a major part of the job. When on duty firefighters live in close proximity with one another. They might on occasion get on each other's nerves. Expect to be questioned about your approach to others and how you might deal with an annoying or possibly inappropriate colleague.

Fitting into the culture of the Fire Service

Firefighters wear uniforms and carry out orders. The service is a lot less militaristic than it used to be but it is still hierarchical. Be sure to identify things that you have done in the past that demonstrate your ability to work under such a regime.

Doing the job safely

The job necessarily involves the taking of risks. But firefighters are never cavalier about their personal safety, or that of their colleagues. Risks are assessed and managed, and the authority to which you apply will want to investigate your approach towards health and safety, and risk-taking in particular.

The preventative work of the Fire Service

It is better to ensure that a fire does not occur in the first place. To some extent, having to go to an emergency implies a failure: the failure to prevent an accident from occurring. Nowadays much of the work of a firefighter is concerned with preventative measures designed to avert an emergency.

Firefighters have always attended schools and public events to promote public safety. In recent years this work has been greatly extended. You must be aware of what it involves and consider what you may have done to demonstrate your suitability for this important aspect of the job, as this may help you to make a strong impression in the firefighter recruitment process.

Why equality of opportunities is so important

What is equality of opportunity?

Equality of opportunity means that people are allowed the same chance to take up education or employment opportunities, or to be protected by organizations such as the Fire Service, and not be excluded from these opportunities on the basis of birth, nationality, religion, race, gender, political belief, sexual preference or disability.

Equality of opportunity means equal treatment and respect. Nothing should prevent people from gaining access to services or employment if their talents, experience and achievements fit the requirements of the position. And someone should get the job, promotion or place on a training course only if they can demonstrate the talent, necessary experience and achievement.

How can you show that you are committed to equality of opportunity?

An effective policy of equality is entrenched in day-to-day working practices. What you do in work on a day-to-day basis therefore can be used as an example to demonstrate your commitment to equality. This means that you demonstrate such a commitment if you treat customers fairly and with respect and provide a service irrespective of the customers' birth, nationality, religion, race, gender, political belief, sexual preference or disability. You demonstrate a commitment to equality if you help ensure the workplace is free from discrimination, bullying or harassment.

If you have undertaken voluntary work in your local community, then you have demonstrated a commitment to equality if you helped members of excluded groups to gain access to services. It might be, for example, playing sports with young people at risk of offending, or giving an elderly neighbour a lift to the polling station on election night or to the doctor's surgery.

The Fire Service is determined to serve all members of our communities irrespective of their race, religion, gender or sexual orientation. It is also determined to serve people both rich and poor. The most disadvantaged people in our society are more likely to require the services of the Fire Service. National statistics show that people who live alone, the elderly, some members of ethnic minority communities and people who do not speak English are more likely to be the victims of a fire-related accident. If the service is to succeed in its commitment to serve all members of our communities, and if it is to succeed in preventing fires, then it must work especially hard to reach out to the members of society who are at most risk of being the victim of a fire. Very often these are the hardest people to communicate with, and in some instances the people who are most likely to mistrust the motives of the service and a firefighter.

Let me illustrate this point, because it is a very important one. Consider a single man over 60 years of age living alone on a low income who smokes and drinks. In every street there is probably someone who fits this description, and national statistics demonstrate that such an individual is far more likely to suffer a fire in his home. He may not have a smoke alarm, and if he does it may not have been tested for some time. His home may be in a state of disrepair, the electrics may be old and he may rely for warmth on unsafe electric heaters. The fire may occur because he falls asleep while smoking and the burning cigarette starts a blaze. Something may drop onto the electric fire or an electric short may occur. The Fire Service spends a great deal of time responding to accidents of this type in the homes of single men. Before you apply to become a firefighter, visit your fire station and find out what the service does in an effort to promote fire safety to such people.

Ask yourself what else the Fire Service can do to safeguard people who live alone. Find out why the elderly or some members of ethnic minority communities may be more likely to suffer a fire in their homes, and learn how the Fire Service in your area is promoting fire safety in order to try to prevent these fires.

Keeping the trust of the public

To do its job well the Fire Service needs the support and trust of the community it serves. To promote fire safety, the service must reach out to people from all sections of the community and all local businesses. It relies on people who run businesses to inform it when dangerous substances are stored or used in a manufacturing process. It relies on the public to inform it of an emergency when one occurs, and not to block fire escapes and access points for fire engines.

A commitment to diversity

You are very likely to be asked about diversity and expected to be able to give examples of when you demonstrated a commitment to it.

What is diversity?

Diversity is about realizing the value of different backgrounds. A diverse group of people working together has advantages over a group of people drawn from, for example, the same race, gender or personal background. A broad range of life experiences, different points of view and ways of seeing things generate the best solutions to problems. A diverse group working together towards a common objective brings a broad range of strengths and accomplishments.

A commitment to diversity means that you don't just tolerate difference but you treasure it and recognize how valuable it can be.

How can you show that you are committed to diversity?

If you went to a multicultural school, you may well look back to that experience as providing rich opportunities to learn from the differences. Did you learn from students from other cultural backgrounds about their religious festivals and traditions? If you did and you look back to that experience positively, then you have a commitment to diversity and all you need do is describe it so that others can credit you with it.

If you have worked for a company with staff drawn from a wide range of backgrounds and ethnic origins, you ought to be able to describe a good many situations where the diversity of your colleagues brought an energy to the task at hand that would otherwise not have been present.

Education and work are probably the most common examples of where commitment to diversity are found, but any number of other situations will do equally well. Any will do so long as they illustrate that you not only tolerate diversity but know it brings advantage and is therefore highly desirable.

Find out more about diversity by searching on the internet and reading the diversity and inclusion policies of major organizations. Google 'diversity policy' for example, and of course search for the diversity policy of the fire authority to which you are applying.

Our diverse and multicultural communities

In many of our cities the communities are diverse in terms of cultures and languages. This diversity makes them vibrant, interesting places but it also makes the work of the Fire Service more complex. Set yourself the task of finding ways that the Fire Service can, for example, effectively promote smoke alarms in a community where perhaps 100 languages are spoken. If the majority of the people who live in a district do not speak English as a first language, then how do you think the Fire Service can ensure that they hear about fire safety, learn about its role and the service it provides, and know who to contact in an emergency? Make sure you can answer these sorts of question before you attend the assessment day.

Before you apply to be a firefighter, find out about the community that you hope to serve, and learn what the fire authority does to promote fire safety and awareness of its services. You can find information about an area from, for example, the website of the local authority and the reference section of a local library. Read the information available and build a picture of the people who live there and the sort of community it is. Is the area rural or urban, for example? Are there large ethnic minority communities and if so what are they? What facilities are available for people who suffer disabilities? Where are the social centres, churches, mosques or temples? If you can, visit the area and drop by at one of the fire stations. The firefighters at the station should be happy to speak to you and answer a few questions (they may not have sufficient time to answer all you might ask, and obviously if there is an emergency they may not be able to spare you any time at all). Pick up any leaflets that are available and see for yourself if there is a banner or notice board outside promoting community safety.

At appropriate points in the recruitment process, ensure that you can describe what involvement you have had in your local community, and try to draw a parallel between the community in which you live and the area in which the fire authority operates. If you speak another language in addition to English, then include this information on your application form. If you have a personal knowledge of a minority culture, then remember to mention this when the occasion arises. At interview, positively discuss features of that culture, for example its religious festivals or cultural attitudes towards the standing of women or elders.

If you have had experience of serving people from a diversity of cultures and backgrounds, then be sure to refer to this experience at an appropriate point in your application.

Serving people with disabilities

The advice, information and assistance provided by a firefighter must be appropriate for all people, including those with disabilities and the profoundly disabled. It is important not to think that it is only people who require a wheelchair that have disabilities, although of course this is an important group of people. The work of the Fire Service must be adapted to suit the needs of many different types of disability. People who are deaf or blind, for example, will require information to be communicated in very specific ways. In an emergency, the help that firefighters offer will need to be adapted to best suit the circumstances of the people they are helping. In an emergency you must be prepared for the unexpected and be able to deal with it. If you are evacuating a train, for example, then it is very likely that some of the passengers will need assistance. It is also likely that some of the passengers will not be able to hear or understand your spoken instructions.

Your application will be greatly enhanced if you are able to refer to previous experience of supporting people with disabilities. Consider attending an evening class in sign language (the language used by the deaf). If through your work you can attend a training course in awareness of people with disabilities, then be sure to ask to attend it; alternatively you could undertake some voluntary work through which you can gain insight into the needs of people with disabilities. If any member of your immediate family suffers from a disability, then be sure to refer to this experience to illustrate your suitability for the role of a firefighter.

Serving hard-to-reach groups

The homeless, people who are dependent on illegal drugs, people living in fear of deportation from the UK and people who earn a living through illegal activities – these people also from time to time need the assistance of the Fire Service. Yet they are understandably very hard to reach in terms of promoting fire safety. Even if the opportunity arises for a firefighter to talk to someone from one of these groups, they have many other concerns that they view as more pressing than fire safety. Obviously, someone who has nowhere to sleep really does not need information on smoke alarms! Even when the Fire Service is able to reach people from these groups, they may be suspicious of the motive. Their language and actions may be challenging. The Fire Service will assist all members of the community irrespective of their status, lifestyle or abode and no matter how challenging their behaviour may seem. If you have had any experience of members of these groups or if your work has brought you into contact with them, then be sure to describe this where the opportunity arises during your application. Try to find out how the Fire Service serves such members of your community. Give some thought as to how the service might better reach members of these groups to promote fire safety.

The Fire Service and crimes involving fire

Unfortunately the number of cases of arson (deliberately started fires) has increased in recent years. Some of these fires are started by young people who have not thought through the consequences of their actions, and the Fire Service is keen to try to explain to as many young people as possible why playing with fire is so dangerous. One very effective method is to park a fire engine at the location of an act of arson and ensure that firefighters talk to the people in the area. The firefighters make no allegations and do not try to find out who started the fire; they simply talk to as many local people as possible, explain what happened and stress how dangerous it is. They hand out leaflets in an effort to ensure that it does not happen again. Of course young people are not responsible for all incidents of arson; many cases are acts of criminal intent where the perpetrators know very well what they are doing. In these instances the firefighters deal with the fire with their usual professionalism, report the incident to the police and leave the criminal investigation to them. The police and the Fire Service are entirely different organizations and this division helps ensure that firefighters are seen by the public as simply interested in protecting the public from danger and providing assistance in emergencies.

Some of the things it takes to be a firefighter

Demonstrate that you possess the qualities of a firefighter

There is no particular prior experience that qualifies you to be a firefighter. There are serving firefighters who prior to joining the service were full-time carers, part-time students or unemployed, or who served in the armed services or had only ever undertaken unpaid voluntary work, only worked in an office or on a building site in one of the trades. In fact almost any past is acceptable, and in any fire station you will meet firefighters drawn from almost every walk of life. Certain experiences will help your application and you should set about gaining experience that will boost your chances of success (see below). But it is important to understand that to a large extent it is not what you have done but how you present your past in interviews and on the application form that will determine whether or not you are successful. You must describe your past in terms of the qualities and responsibilities relevant to the role of a firefighter.

A great many very good candidates fail to do this and so fail in their application.

Show a lifelong commitment to maintaining your knowledge, skills and fitness

Firefighters must demonstrate a commitment to maintaining their knowledge, skills and fitness throughout their career. The Fire Service will be looking for evidence on the application form and at interview that you have done this before and that you continue to do it. No matter what you have done in the past, you should be able to describe it in a way that demonstrates that you have kept abreast of new developments through training or reading (knowledge), that you have continued to keep your skills up to the standard required (again through training or through gaining qualifications) and that you maintain your fitness through exercise or sport or both.

Tell them the obvious

It is important to state the obvious. It may, for example, seem obvious to you that you have maintained your knowledge, skills and fitness and always will do. You may play a sport at a high level and it is obvious that you cannot do that unless you maintain your knowledge, skills and fitness. The person marking your application form or judging you at interview will not give you the credit for having this quality unless you point it out directly. Consider the following two answers to the question:

> 'Have you ever needed to maintain knowledge, skills and fitness?'

The answer that misses the point: 'Yes, when I represented my county in athletics for four years.'

The answer that spells it out: 'Yes, when I represented my county in athletics. This required me to train every morning five days a week for over four years and I still train. I attended regular *training camps where I was coached in the latest techniques and I continually worked to develop my style and technique in order to remain competitive.'*

If you were to have represented your county in a sport it would be a great achievement but alone it does not demonstrate anything relevant to the job of a firefighter. You must spell it out and explain that relevance both in your written answers and in your spoken answers to the questions asked of you.

Do not worry if you have not done anything as impressive as playing a sport at a high level. However, you must be prepared to pull out relevant qualities from your past experiences that demonstrate you have what it takes to become a successful firefighter.

Show that you can see a job through to the end

A firefighter must be someone who sees a job through to the end, someone who can show determination and endurance. As previously mentioned the application process is long and demanding. You are very likely to have to apply a number of times before you succeed. When you experience failure you will have to find the strength of character to apply again. These are all qualities that make for a good firefighter. Realize that the application process is testing you to see if you have what it takes to be a firefighter. Make sure you can describe occasions when you have seen a difficult job through to the end.

Prove that you can communicate effectively

A firefighter must be able to communicate well with both colleagues and the general public. This has become a really important part of the job and it is also an important part of the application process. The Fire Service expects you to be able to describe your past in terms that demonstrate your suitability for the role. The selectors expect you to be able to discuss the preventative work of the service. They look carefully to see if you can listen to the contribution of others and contribute to a discussion yourself. At interview they expect you to be able to answer each question and provide further examples if they ask follow-up questions. They do not want you to repeat the same point over again but rather to make a different relevant point or provide another example. Many otherwise good applicants fail because they are not sufficiently well practised at speaking in a group, answering the question posed to them or contributing to a quite complex conversation at interview. If you are one of these applicants then take heart, because you can learn these skills and with the right sort of practice you will greatly improve your performance in any group exercise and the interview.

Prepare thoroughly for the interview

The secret of a good interview is preparation. Be prepared to provide up to three different examples in response to the questions you expect to be asked. You can to a large extent anticipate the questions, or at least the likely subject of the questions, and prepare potential answers. This sort of preparation is a bit like doing some of the thinking up front so that during the interview you can adapt what you have prepared to best suit the question or follow-up question.

Take, for example, the common question: 'When have you had to solve a problem?' Your answer can be drawn from any aspect of your past, including time spent raising a family, at school, college or work. Once you have answered the question, the selectors may ask you to describe another occasion when you have solved a problem. They prefer that you draw the second example from another aspect of your life. So if you used an example from work to answer the first question, then try to avoid giving another example from your work; instead give an example from your home life, social or sporting life, or your involvement in your community. Occasionally you will be asked to provide a third example, so make sure that you are able to provide three examples to all of the questions that you anticipate being asked. Each example should be drawn from a different aspect of your past that you have already referred to in your application form.

Practise the written tests

A firefighter must be numerate, observant when under pressure and able to interpret quite complex information. These skills are tested in the written tests. It is essential to practise before attempting the real tests so be sure to work through all the material provided in this book. Practice will help you to demonstrate your true potential and increase your chances of passing. If necessary obtain the recommended further reading too. Keep practising until you are confident that you will stand out from the other applicants.

Attend fit

To succeed in the firefighter recruitment process you must demonstrate a high level of physical fitness and pass a series of work-related physical tests. Do not underestimate how fit you need to be to pass these tests, and do not make the mistake of overestimating the level of your current fitness. If a few years ago you used to play a great deal of sport or ran a marathon in good time, you might well have been fit enough to pass the firefighter selection process then, but are you still fit enough? Do you still train to maintain your fitness? How often do you train each week? Do you push yourself in these training sessions? Be prepared to spend weeks or months building up your physical fitness in order to reach the required level. Aim to do more than just pass the fitness tests. Set yourself the challenge of doing really well in them. Some of the other candidates will be very fit indeed and you should aim to do almost as well as the best who attend on the same day.

Other things to consider

Applicants that are representative of the communities they serve

The Fire Service is keen that the firefighters it recruits represent the communities they serve. This means that the Fire Service would like to recruit more people who live locally and who are drawn from the various communities that are present in the area.

This is why you should set out to find out about the community you hope to serve and why you should promote that knowledge and any personal experience you have of that community.

If you describe your ethnic origin as belonging to an ethnic minority group currently under-represented in the Fire Service, then before you submit your application there may be extra help and encouragement available to you. This extra assistance is very likely to stop once you have submitted your application to be a firefighter, so contact your local Fire Service recruit team early on to enquire if such support is available, and make the most of it prior to making your application.

While the service would prefer to recruit people who are representative of the community, it is committed to a policy of recruitment on the basis of merit. You can be assured that it will select the best candidates in terms of how they perform in the recruitment process, irrespective of their race or ethnic origin.

More female firefighters

There are not enough female firefighters, so the Fire Service wants to encourage more women to apply. In some areas there are special training courses that help women prepare for their applications, helping them to demonstrate their full potential. These courses are usually really worthwhile and you can gain a lot personally from taking part. To establish if such a course is offered in your area, call the recruitment team at your local fire authority and ask whether such a course is available or planned in the future.

Holding a driving licence

You may well need to hold a full UK driving licence before you can be appointed as a firefighter. You may hold a provisional licence while you apply but your final appointment may be dependent on your obtaining a full licence. Check the information sent to you with the application forms or with the authority to which you are applying to see if this is the case.

If you have a criminal conviction

Not all criminal convictions will exclude you from becoming a firefighter. It will depend on the type of conviction and the time that has passed since you were convicted. A full police check is made of all applicant firefighters before an offer of employment is made. In some cases an offer of employment is made subject to a satisfactory police check. If you have a conviction then the best policy to adopt is a completely open one. Contact the recruitment team at the fire authority to whom you have applied and discuss your conviction with one of the team. They should be able to indicate whether this will be a problem or not.

Your medical health

Before you are appointed as a firefighter you undergo a quite extensive medical examination. This process is expensive (the Fire Service pays, there is no cost to you) and for this reason the fire authority leaves the medical until the end of the application process. Thus the authority does not incur the cost of medicals in the case of applicants who do not pass the written tests or assessment day.

There are some quite common medical conditions that regrettably will mean that you cannot become a firefighter. These include some cases of asthma and a number of skin conditions. Poor eyesight or impaired hearing may also exclude you from the service. If you fear that you suffer a medical condition that might prevent you from becoming a firefighter, then it is best to find out sooner rather than later. You would not want to go through all the stages of the recruitment process only to fail at the very end over something that you could have established earlier on was going to exclude you. For this reason, if you fear that the medical might be a problem, it might be best to discuss your plans to apply to become a firefighter with your GP. Otherwise mention your medical concern to the fire authority recruitment team and see if they can provide any guidance. Ultimately only the Fire Service doctor can decide if you are fit for the job, but the advice of others can help you decide whether you want to take the risk of applying.

If you suffer a disability

The work of a firefighter obviously excludes many people who suffer from a disability from holding down the job. However, there are some disabilities that will not affect your ability to do the job but that might mean that you need things organized differently during the recruitment process. An example is dyslexia. If you suffer such a disability then notify the fire authority at the first opportunity and give them the opportunity to accommodate your needs. They may, for example, allow you extra time to complete the written tests or make some other appropriate accommodation depending on your circumstances. Note that before they do this they are likely to require proof that you suffer the disability; if this is the case and you do not already hold such proof, then you need to straight away set about organizing an official assessment by a professional. The cost of this assessment is very likely to be yours. Once again the best thing to do is to call the recruitment team at the fire authority to which you have applied or plan to apply, and discuss your situation with them.

Open days and information days organized by the Fire Service

Find out if your local fire authority organizes open days at fire stations or if the recruitment team holds information days. These are really interesting events at which you will obtain a great deal of useful information.

Information on the web

The various fire authorities around the UK provide a great deal of information about the role of the Fire Service on their websites. It is well worth spending a few hours surfing the various sites and familiarizing yourself with the latest initiatives and facts.

Help at mikebryon.com

Many candidates need to undertake extensive practice before they pass the firefighter recruitment process. If you are finding it difficult to identify further practice material, or if you would like further advice on a specific point about the firefighter recruitment process, then by all means e-mail me at help@mikebryon.com.

The recruitment process for firefighters does sometimes change, and consequently this book may no longer cover all aspects of the process. If this is the case, do e-mail me at the above address and I will direct you to any sources I know for the latest advice and practice exercises.

Experience that may improve your prospects

There are a great many things that you can learn or volunteer to do that may improve your prospects of succeeding in your goal to become a firefighter. There is no guarantee, but the suggestions below might well help you to succeed in your aim. They definitely will mean that you can refer to additional and valuable experience in support of your application. They are not listed in order of importance. You should only consider those that genuinely interest you and that will fill a gap in your experience or skills.

Useful skills to learn

All firefighters are expected to show a lifelong commitment to maintaining their skills and knowledge; if your application is thin on details of training, courses or qualifications, then now is the time to put that right. The acquisition of any skill or knowledge will support your application and a course of training need not lead to a qualification to count. You can learn part time, in the evenings, online or even teach yourself something – it will all count.

- Learn a minority language spoken in your community.
  You may not need to become fluent in a language for it to be

judged an asset. Attending an evening class or learning online a minority language spoken in the community in which you wish to serve would help make your application stand out. The BBC provides free language training. To get started, visit www.how-to-learn-any-language.com and www.bbc.co.uk/language.

- Gain a qualification in sports.
  All firefighters are expected to show a lifelong commitment to maintaining their fitness as well as their skills and knowledge. Why not look into combining these two requirements and gaining a qualification in sport? There are many possibilities; for example, you can train to become a coach or referee. There are qualifications in sports leadership and management. Visit the website of the sporting body responsible for the sport you most enjoy; also visit, for example, www.sportsleaders.org/our-awardsqualifications.

- Get qualified as a mentor.
  Mentors provide advice and guidance to young people, people facing a challenge or families. A mentor will make a long-term commitment to keep in touch with the individuals and meet them regularly. Most local authorities have someone whose job it is to coordinate volunteers, and if you contact that person in your area they should be able to suggest a number of charitable organizations that provide mentoring and will train you in mentoring skills.

- Learn British sign language.
  British sign language and sign-supported English are both official minority languages in the UK. To find out where to learn them or to join an online course visit www.british-sign.co.uk.

- Attend training in equal opportunities and/or awareness of the needs of people with disabilities.
  Many employers have staff development budgets and training policies, and those usually permit staff to apply for training. It is unlikely that the policy will encourage you to apply for training in a subject unrelated to your work; however, training in equality or disability awareness is very likely to be judged as relevant. So, ask your human resource team if there is a staff development fund and apply.

● Enrol on a course to gain a qualification or further qualification relevant to your current work.

There are thousands of occupational training providers across the UK both public and private, and one local to you will surely offer a course relevant to your current work. Gaining a qualification in your area of employment will impress your current employer and it will also enhance your application to become a firefighter. For a huge listing of courses see www.hotcourses.com.

● Enrol on a course for adults in, for example, numeracy, communication, IT skills or customer service.

It does not matter where you live, you can learn new skills at your own pace and broken down into bite-sized units. To find out more, visit www.learndirect.co.uk.

● Undertake training or a course of study at a local college.

There are all sorts of evening classes, part-time courses and short courses of learning to choose from. To find something that interests you, search at the BBC's course finder: www.bbc.co.uk/learning.

● Learn online.

If your personal circumstances will not allow you to train in a college or classroom, then investigate the incredible range of subjects and courses offered online. Search, for example, first aid, sports, maths and foreign languages at www.bbc.co.uk/learning/onlinecourses and www.learndirect.co.uk.

Putting something back

One person can make a difference. In fact, there are very many ways you can make the world a better place and at the same time improve your chances of succeeding as an applicant firefighter. Voluntary work brings benefits for the volunteers as well as the community they serve; many volunteers are provided with training. They can work just a few hours a week, a day a month or full-time. The choice is yours. Normally expenses such as travel costs are paid and often a lunch allowance is provided. Most local authorities have volunteer coordinators who can help match you to a voluntary position. The Department of Employment's jobcentre personal advisers may also help you find voluntary work. Below are examples, all unpaid, that give a flavour of the variety of opportunities that exist:

- Driver for a charity for the elderly. Mobility is a major obstacle to the elderly and a large number of organizations organize volunteer drivers. If you have access to a car and like to drive, then your local authority should have a volunteers' adviser who will put you in touch with a coordinator. See www.rotary.org.

- Translator/interpreter for an inner city community project. If you speak a minority language then your assistance will always be welcome with translation and acting as an interpreter. This will keep your language skills sharp and allow you to meet people from that linguistic community. You can find information on these sorts of project at, for example, www.islingtonvolunteeringassociation.org/contact.php or at www.mind.org.uk.

- Listening volunteer. A large number of volunteers give up their time to listen and offer sympathy and sound advice to people suffering a personal crisis. Charities active in this field provide training and support to their volunteers. For further information see www.volunteerscotland.org.uk or www.samaritans.org.

- Helpline volunteer for a child death charity. Staffing help lines is a major area of voluntary work. If you have personal experience of the area of work of the charity, then you are best qualified to offer such support. Volunteers may also find that it helps them too in that they feel some small good can come from their traumatic experience. You can find out more at www.childdeathhelpline.org.uk or at www.ndcs.org.uk.

- Volunteer friend for prisoners and their family. A number of charities provide support to both prisoners and their families by putting them in touch with friends. Such friends will listen, correspond and help where they can. It can make a huge difference to the individuals concerned and may help to reduce the likelihood of re-offending on release. There are also organizations that provide support for the victims of crime. You can read more at www.pffs.org.uk/volunteers.

- Clean-up-your-area campaigners and volunteers. If there is something about your neighbourhood that you think could be improved and you have thought 'Why doesn't someone do something about it?' – then perhaps it's time you took the initiative. You can lead by example, roll up your sleeves and make a start yourself. You may well find that others join you. Alternatively, you can recruit others and between you set about the task. Such groups have formed to clear up litter or slow down traffic for example. Find out how you can play an active role in your community by visiting www.csv.org.uk.

- Special police officer. The police forces in the UK (including the transport police) recruit and use volunteer support police officers. Special constables receive training and uniforms and work alongside a member of the police force at, for example, public events and town centres on a Saturday night. Many use voluntary work as a 'special' to support their application for a position as a police officer or firefighter. You can find further details at www.policecouldyou.co.uk/specials.

- Volunteer handyman/woman. If you are a DIY enthusiast, then there is a constant need for skills in the home of the elderly or volunteering to help tenants of housing associations. You can find out how to be a volunteer in your community at, for example, www.volunteering.org.uk.

- Sports mentor for youth. If sport is your thing, then there is a great deal of good you can do organizing or getting involved in activities for young people. A number of charities focus on organizing such events for young people believed to be at risk of offending, hoping that if young people are encouraged to become involved in sport they are less likely to offend. Find out about this type of voluntary work at www.youthsporttrust.org.

- Dog walker for elderly neighbours. Many elderly people living alone greatly enjoy the companionship of a dog but are unable to exercise it sufficiently due to restricted mobility. A neighbour who is happy to walk the dog is doing them both a service, and the walker might just stay a little fitter too.

- Archaeology fieldworker. Volunteers make up a sizeable number of the individuals involved in the vast majority of archaeological digs. They work under the direction of the site archaeologist and attend specialist briefings on the discoveries made. You can find out more at, for example, www.archaeologyfieldwork.com.

- Provide leadership skills training for young people living in deprived communities. Leadership skills training is about empowering people to help themselves and the communities in which they live. Such training is provided in many communities that are judged to be disadvantaged in terms of access to employment or education. See, for example, www.preset.org.

- Assembling flat-pack furniture for re-housed families. If you are mobile and handy, then offering to assemble flat-pack furniture for re-housed families is a way in which you can contribute to your community. Housing associations or local authority housing departments will let you know if they use volunteers for this role. You can browse volunteer opportunities at www.timebank.org.uk. Or you could propose helping with flat-pack furniture at, for example, www.wrvs.org.uk.

- Overseas volunteer conservation fieldworker. There are many overseas national parks or sites of special scientific interest that rely on volunteers to help with maintenance and management. This can involve such work as helping to remove invasive species, building or repairing fences, planting native species, leading groups of visitors and fundraising. Find out more at, for example, www.earthwatch.org.

- Volunteer coastguard. There are charitable bodies that organize volunteer coastguards to provide help in the event of a maritime accident or shipwreck. The volunteer staff watch from sites, monitor the radio and patrol inshore in small vessels. The largest of these organizations in the UK and Ireland is the RNLI, which provides all-weather offshore, as well as inshore, lifeboats. The UK coastal watch system has a website at www.mcga.gov.uk.

● Volunteer paramedic. There are a number of charities that provide paramedics and first aid at public events. To become a volunteer and receive first-class training in these life-saving skills contact, for example, the St John Ambulance service.

● Volunteer at the Olympic Games. It is not just the athletes who are amateurs in the Olympics; representatives of sports governing bodies, judges and invigilators are all volunteers too. For the 2012 games visit www.london2012.com/get-involved/volunteering.

● Saturday morning soccer team coach. A great army of people help organize and invigilate in weekend amateur sporting events for both adults and children. Get along to your local teams and ask how you might help.

● Local community conservation fieldworker. Educational sites and urban sites of scientific interest use volunteers to help maintain their biodiversity and sustainability. Your local authority volunteer coordinator will have details.

● Soldier in the Territorial Army. The Territorial Army is staffed by volunteers who train at weekends and evenings and attend longer training events where they exercise alongside the regular army. Members of the Territorial Army go on active service and in times of crises are called on to help defend the nation. Find out more at www.armyjobs.mod.uk.

● Adult literacy or numeracy tutor. The formal education system fails many people who leave compulsory education without a sufficient grasp of the basic skills of reading, writing and mathematics. Some of these individuals have to be encouraged to address that failure as adults and will work for many months learning these key skills. Most of the teachers who assist them in this are volunteers. You can e-mail the Basic Skills Agency at: enquiries@basic-skills.co.uk.

- Mountain rescue or ski patrol. In areas of the world where people practise the leisure pursuits of mountaineering or skiing, there are volunteers who patrol or will go in search of someone lost or injured on the slopes. For inspiration visit www.mountain.rescue.org.uk/contact-us and www.mrc-scotland.org.uk.

The recruitment process

While a fire authority will receive thousands of applications, the number of vacancies it has for firefighters may be in the tens. In the case of the smaller authorities there may be only a handful of vacancies. The application process will include all or most of the following stages:

- application form;
- attitudinal questionnaires;
- written tests;
- interview;
- team exercise;
- physical tests;
- work-based physical tests;
- medical examination;
- references.

The rest of this book is arranged around these features of the recruitment process with advice, tips and insights provided for each. It provides exercises and hundreds of practice questions to complete in preparation for the recruitment process.

CHAPTER 2

The application forms and questionnaire about your attitude to work

All fire authorities will require you to complete a set of application forms, and may require you to complete initial and supplementary forms as you progress through the selection process.

Getting hold of a set of forms may be harder than you expect, and this may represent the first of many challenges. This is because so many candidates register an interest that the authorities feel obliged to limit the number of forms sent out. They may do this by, for example, issuing applications on a first-come first-served basis until the agreed number is reached. So register your interest straight away. Alternatively, they may issue applications only to applicants selected randomly by computer from the total list of all initial applicants.

If you receive an application form, look after it! If you lose it or spill coffee over it you are unlikely to be offered a replacement. It will comprise more than one part and you will be required to complete and return all sections. So make one or more photocopies of the blank forms and put the original away in a safe place. Write your answers on the copies and only fill in the real form when you are completely happy with all your responses and you have carefully checked your answers.

Make a note of the closing date by which the completed form must be submitted. Read carefully and keep all the information sent with it. Make sure you complete the entries using a black pen if that is what the instructions require, and complete them in very neat handwriting with no spelling mistakes. Only submit the original forms, as photocopies are unlikely to be accepted.

Most candidates spend far too little time on the application forms; they fail to give proper consideration to the questions and do not think carefully enough about their answers. Take the application forms very seriously – they may well represent the stage when most applicants are rejected. It is likely that, for example, if 3,000 application forms are returned only 1,000 applicants will be invited to the next stage of the process. The rest will be rejected on the grounds that the information they provided did not meet the criteria of the fire authority.

Your application will be judged by what you write in response to the questions and the accuracy with which you complete the forms. You must answer every question, and what you state must be truthful, relevant and clear.

Make a copy of your completed form and keep it for future reference. You might be asked about your answers at the interview stage and, for example, be asked to explain what you meant or to provide further information.

Advice and tips on completing the questions

The application forms will comprise a pack of information and forms that can be divided into two styles of question. You need to approach each type of question differently so I have treated them separately below. Read the advice and tips relating to each sort and complete the exercises before you attempt to complete the real application forms.

Questions relating to your personal details

You must provide answers to a series of questions that allow the authority to confirm that you meet the minimum criteria for the role (your application pack will explain these criteria). You are also required to provide details so that the authority is able to correspond with you, and to help enable the authority to establish whether it is attracting applications from all sections of the community.

These are the most straightforward of the question types and amount simply to requests for personal details and dates. They ask for your full name, date of birth, nationality, ethnic origin, medical history, work history, qualifications, details of any criminal convictions and so on. Be sure to answer every question and provide all the details requested. If you omit any information, then the authority may not be able to confirm that you meet the minimum criteria. They will not contact you to ask for further details but will simply reject your application on the grounds that you have not provided sufficient information.

Be as accurate as you can in providing these details. Rather than trying to recall from memory the names of your qualifications, for example, find the certificates and copy them down exactly. Establish the exact month and year that you left one place of work and the exact month and year that you began work at the next. If there is a gap between the dates then detail what you were doing in that period. It is perfectly all right to say, for example, that you were seeking employment or were a home maker or carer for that period, if that was in fact the case.

Much of the information that you provide is double-checked later, so do not be tempted to omit information that you feel might count against you. If you are worried about disclosing some information, call the recruitment section of the fire authority and ask for further guidance.

Remember to keep a copy of your completed forms and read through them before you attend the assessment centre later in the recruitment process. At interview you may be asked questions about the detail you have provided, and it would make rather a poor impression if you could not recall what you had written.

Questions about things you have done

These questions require you to write brief statements about your experience or interests that demonstrate your suitability for the position of a firefighter. Typically you are provided with a space in which you can write approximately 100–170 words in answer to each question posed.

Lots of people find this part of the application form difficult or do not make a very good job of it. There is no limit on how much time you may spend preparing your answers, so take the trouble to do it properly.

Take your time over this type of question. You will not come up with the best answer on your first attempt. So think carefully about each of the questions and how it relates to the role and responsibilities of a firefighter. Set out to make every word count.

When answering this sort of question you can use examples from any sphere of your life, so do not limit what you say to what you have done at work, school or college for example. Be sure to refer to any voluntary work or involvement with your local community. And if you speak a second language or have experience of supporting people with a disability or people who suffer mental health problems, make that clear on the form.

It is important that you do not use the same example in answer to all the questions. This is a common mistake and one that results in a lot of failed applications. Do not refer to your work in response to every question. If you only refer to one aspect of your life it gives the impression that it is the only thing you have done. The person scoring your answers will not give you more than one point for repeating the same experience.

Make sure that you have an answer to every question and make use of all the space provided. Be sure that what you write is relevant to the job of a firefighter and answers the question. Try thinking of more than one experience that you could use to answer the question. Then decide which of them is best. Test your answers out on friends and family and encourage them to suggest things you have done that you might use.

There is no need to exaggerate your past or invent things. Lots of everyday, ordinary experiences will serve well to illustrate that you have the experience, skills and knowledge to be a firefighter.

Make sure that your answer forms a proper series of sentences that read well. Eliminate spelling mistakes. It helps if you write your answers out first on a computer as you can then use the spelling and grammar checker to get them exactly right. Once you are happy with your statement copy it onto the application form.

Exercise 1

Write 100–170 word statements in response to the following questions. In some instances I have asked you to describe up to three situations illustrating the same point. Get someone to read your answers and, where you have provided more than one example, ask them to identify which they consider the best. This exercise will serve as useful preparatory work for the real application forms. It is also valuable preparation for the interview.

1   Describe a situation where you had to start doing something in a different way from usual.

2 Describe three occasions when you worked collaboratively as part of a team to successfully complete something.

Occasion 1

Occasion 2

Occasion 3

3 Detail any voluntary or community work that you have undertaken and how you think this experience might help make you a better firefighter.

4 Describe something you have successfully completed when working alone while following written guidelines.

5 Describe three occasions when you have worked together with others to solve a practical problem.

Occasion 1

Occasion 2

Occasion 3

6   Describe a situation where you have undertaken tasks in hot, cramped or dirty conditions.

7   Describe three occasions when you have accomplished a task while working collaboratively with people from different ethnic backgrounds, ages and genders.

Occasion 1

Occasion 2

Occasion 3

8   In 100 words describe the community in which you live.

9   Give two accounts of how you have dealt with stressful situations.

Account 1

Account 2

10 Describe two situations where you have had to show commitment.

Situation 1

Situation 2

11 Detail any training you have undertaken that you consider is relevant to the role of a firefighter.

12 Describe how you keep yourself physically fit.

13 Describe your attitude towards carrying out the instructions of a person in authority who may be younger than yourself.

14 Describe two situations when you have taken responsibility for your own personal development.

Situation 1

Situation 2

Questions about your personality

Under the structure of the first national standards, questions about your personality and attitude towards certain situations formed part of the application form. Under the new structure, the situational questions are taken after the written tests when you attend the test centre. You will find lots of practice for the situational awareness paper in Chapter 3.

The questionnaire that investigates your personality requires you to indicate whether you agree or disagree with a statement or whether or not it is a true statement about you. You may be asked if you strongly agree or disagree or only partially agree or disagree.

Many people rush these questions and do not give them sufficient consideration. Take them seriously because the answers you give will be used to decide if your application should be accepted or rejected.

You should answer the questions truthfully and keep at the front of your mind the context of the question. You are applying to be a firefighter and it is in this context that you are answering the questions. With each question ask yourself: 'As an applicant firefighter how would I respond in that situation?' Take the first example of the practice questions below: 'Is honesty always the best policy?' You should be able to answer this question positively. You might be able to think up some unlikely situation when honesty is not always the best policy, say to protect a child from what might otherwise be a very hurtful situation, and for this reason you might conclude that in some circumstances dishonesty is sometimes acceptable. But this would be a totally wrong response in the context of the question. Such an unlikely situation would not apply to you in the role of a firefighter. As a firefighter honesty would always be your best policy. A firefighter is placed in a position of high trust and the Fire Service does not want dishonest firefighters.

Responding truthfully to the questions will sometimes mean that you admit to something that risks counting against you. For example, if you do not speak a second language fluently or if you have never worn a uniform at work, then be prepared to say so.

It is unlikely that a few of these answers will prevent you from being selected for the next stage of the process, but if you lie and it is discovered at interview, your application will be rejected.

Look out for questions that include double negatives. They can be very misleading and you can easily answer them in a way that you did not intend. An example of this sort of question might be:

> 'Do you agree or disagree with the statement: It is not true that I am not over 18 years of age.'

Confusing isn't it. The way to approach this sort of question is to break it down into parts. Begin by answering the factual bit of the question, in this instance: 'I am not over 18 years of age.' To be a firefighter you must be over 18 years so you would most likely disagree with this statement. Now add the 'it is not true' part of the question. This in effect changes your answer from disagreeing to agreeing. You would agree that it is not true that you are not over 18 years of age. If you still find this confusing then don't worry; I have provided lots more practice questions of this sort and you will soon get the hang of these tricky questions.

When answering the questions it is best not to give loads of 'agree strongly' or 'disagree strongly' responses. If you do, you might risk the Fire Service concluding that you are someone with many strongly held opinions who may not easily fit into a team. It is also best not to give too many responses that you neither disagree or agree with a statement, as this might indicate that you find it difficult to make up your mind or commit yourself. By all means agree strongly with a statement such as 'There is no place in work for racism' or 'The Fire Service will assist all members of the community irrespective of their status, lifestyle or abode.' However, don't overdo it and agree or disagree strongly with lots of questions. It is fine to give some of these strongly held or noncommittal responses, but try not to indicate too many.

Exercise 2

Below you will find 100 practice questions that investigate your personality. To each you must indicate whether you agree strongly, agree, neither agree nor disagree, disagree or disagree strongly. Give honest, considered responses to them. Be sure to present yourself as an applicant firefighter. You do this by asking yourself in every instance: 'How would I respond to this question as an applicant firefighter?'

It is important to be consistent in your response. On the real application form the questions return to investigate the same issue a number of times (each is worded slightly differently). You should try to answer these related questions consistently, in other words in the same way. It can be a bit tricky because the questions are not all together but spread out through the body of the questionnaire. To help you practise spotting and consistently answering related questions I have included a good few below; I have spread them out and I have identified them in the answers section.

I have not provided model answers to these questions because in many instances the answers will depend on your personal circumstances. I have provided an explanation to each of the questions indicating the likely way in which the fire authority will interpret it, and have indicated the questions that you should have answered consistently. Note that answering questions consistently does not mean that you should have always agreed or always disagreed with them, but rather that they are investigating your approach to a particular issue and your approach should be consistent (which might mean you agree with one statement but disagree with another).

1   Honesty is always the best policy.

Agree strongly
Agree
Do not agree or disagree
Disagree
Disagree strongly

Answer [   ]

2   To use recreational drugs in the privacy of your own home is a personal matter.

Agree strongly
Agree
Do not agree or disagree
Disagree
Disagree strongly

Answer

3   If someone is shouting and screaming, then it is best to just ignore them.

Agree strongly
Agree
Do not agree or disagree
Disagree
Disagree strongly

Answer

4   If I find I have a different opinion from others, then I usually change the subject and discuss something else.

Agree strongly
Agree
Do not agree or disagree
Disagree
Disagree strongly

Answer

5   Being opinionated is not always a bad thing.

Agree strongly
Agree
Do not agree or disagree
Disagree
Disagree strongly

Answer

6   Knowledge is not power.

Agree strongly
Agree
Do not agree or disagree
Disagree
Disagree strongly

Answer [   ]

7   When a painful decision needs to be taken I would find it impossible to decide.

Agree strongly
Agree
Do not agree or disagree
Disagree
Disagree strongly

Answer [   ]

8   In principle I could carry out a duty that went against my personal beliefs.

Agree strongly
Agree
Do not agree or disagree
Disagree
Disagree strongly

Answer [   ]

9   My work has sometimes involved me explaining things to groups of people.

Agree strongly
Agree
Do not agree or disagree
Disagree
Disagree strongly

Answer [   ]

10 It is wrong to suggest that a compromise is rarely the right decision.

Agree strongly
Agree
Do not agree or disagree
Disagree
Disagree strongly

Answer

11 The fire station cannot be part of the local community like the school or hospital.

Agree strongly
Agree
Do not agree or disagree
Disagree
Disagree strongly

Answer

12 It is best not to upset people by telling them something they do not want to hear.

Agree strongly
Agree
Do not agree or disagree
Disagree
Disagree strongly

Answer

13 I can speak a second language fluently.

Agree strongly
Agree
Do not agree or disagree
Disagree
Disagree strongly

Answer

14 It would be wrong to say that, although I get on with most people, there are nearly always a few people whom I don't much like.

Agree strongly
Agree
Do not agree or disagree
Disagree
Disagree strongly

Answer

15 I am a very active person and I can't concentrate or sit still for very long.

Agree strongly
Agree
Do not agree or disagree
Disagree
Disagree strongly

Answer

16 Everyone from time to time will make mistakes but the important thing is to be up front about them and work together to put them right.

Agree strongly
Agree
Do not agree or disagree
Disagree
Disagree strongly

Answer

17 I don't agree that my actions speak louder than my words.

Agree strongly
Agree
Do not agree or disagree
Disagree
Disagree strongly

Answer

18 Working as part of a team is no more important an aspect of the role of a firefighter than being able to communicate about fire safety to all sections of the community.

Agree strongly
Agree
Do not agree or disagree
Disagree
Disagree strongly

Answer [   ]

19 I am the sort of person who thinks carefully before taking risks.

Agree strongly
Agree
Do not agree or disagree
Disagree
Disagree strongly

Answer [   ]

20 The occasional lie is OK but I generally try to be truthful.

Agree strongly
Agree
Do not agree or disagree
Disagree
Disagree strongly

Answer [   ]

21 I work well when I have to follow clearly defined regulatory procedures.

Agree strongly
Agree
Do not agree or disagree
Disagree
Disagree strongly

Answer [   ]

22   If I knew a colleague was being bullied then I would report it to someone in authority.

Agree strongly
Agree
Do not agree or disagree
Disagree
Disagree strongly

Answer

23   I have always found it very difficult to explain how I personally feel about something.

Agree strongly
Agree
Do not agree or disagree
Disagree
Disagree strongly

Answer

24   It is not advisable not to follow the advice in a safety notice.

Agree strongly
Agree
Do not agree or disagree
Disagree
Disagree strongly

Answer

25   A person who can't speak English can't expect the same level of service as someone who can.

Agree strongly
Agree
Do not agree or disagree
Disagree
Disagree strongly

Answer

26   It is not true that firefighters must constantly train for emergencies and so do not have the time to show local people around the fire station.

Agree strongly
Agree
Do not agree or disagree
Disagree
Disagree strongly

Answer [   ]

27   If there is an attractive woman in the team then it is only natural that the men present will try to impress her.

Agree strongly
Agree
Do not agree or disagree
Disagree
Disagree strongly

Answer [   ]

28   I am happiest when working in an office.

Agree strongly
Agree
Do not agree or disagree
Disagree
Disagree strongly

Answer [   ]

29   It is not true that I take pride in being dogmatic.

Agree strongly
Agree
Do not agree or disagree
Disagree
Disagree strongly

Answer [   ]

30   I would prefer to be my own boss.

Agree strongly
Agree
Do not agree or disagree
Disagree
Disagree strongly

Answer

31   If you make a mistake, it is best to work really hard to put it right and then report it to your employer.

Agree strongly
Agree
Do not agree or disagree
Disagree
Disagree strongly

Answer

32   If your supervisor tells you to do something then you should do it even if you know it is going to be a mistake.

Agree strongly
Agree
Do not agree or disagree
Disagree
Disagree strongly

Answer

33   There are some sorts of people that I just know I am not going to get on with.

Agree strongly
Agree
Do not agree or disagree
Disagree
Disagree strongly

Answer

34   Being brave is not more important to a firefighter than a commitment to stay fit throughout his or her career.

Agree strongly
Agree
Do not agree or disagree
Disagree
Disagree strongly

Answer [   ]

35   I am happy to work nights, weekends and on public holidays.

Agree strongly
Agree
Do not agree or disagree
Disagree
Disagree strongly

Answer [   ]

36   At work I prefer to give orders than receive them.

Agree strongly
Agree
Do not agree or disagree
Disagree
Disagree strongly

Answer [   ]

37   If I do not know someone then I find it very hard to speak to them.

Agree strongly
Agree
Do not agree or disagree
Disagree
Disagree strongly

Answer [   ]

38 It is sometimes clever to make a derisive remark.

Agree strongly
Agree
Do not agree or disagree
Disagree
Disagree strongly

Answer

39 I like to work in an environment where my role and responsibilities are clear.

Agree strongly
Agree
Do not agree or disagree
Disagree
Disagree strongly

Answer

40 Someone who is rude all the time cannot expect the same service as everyone else.

Agree strongly
Agree
Do not agree or disagree
Disagree
Disagree strongly

Answer

41 Too many written procedures don't get in the way of doing a job well.

Agree strongly
Agree
Do not agree or disagree
Disagree
Disagree strongly

Answer

42 If you are right about something then those that hold a different view must be wrong.

Agree strongly
Agree
Do not agree or disagree
Disagree
Disagree strongly

Answer

43 If I say I am going to do something then I do my level best to keep my word.

Agree strongly
Agree
Do not agree or disagree
Disagree
Disagree strongly

Answer

44 It is not true that I feel uncomfortable when given orders.

Agree strongly
Agree
Do not agree or disagree
Disagree
Disagree strongly

Answer

45 It is a fact that women are better at some jobs than men.

Agree strongly
Agree
Do not agree or disagree
Disagree
Disagree strongly

Answer

46   It is not obvious to me that people need to refrain from using bad language at work.

Agree strongly
Agree
Do not agree or disagree
Disagree
Disagree strongly

Answer

47   I put my safety above that of my colleagues.

Agree strongly
Agree
Do not agree or disagree
Disagree
Disagree strongly

Answer

48   If I agree with something someone has said, at an appropriate moment I might well tell them so.

Agree strongly
Agree
Do not agree or disagree
Disagree
Disagree strongly

Answer

49   Even if you know they won't like it, it is best to be up front and tell people what you know.

Agree strongly
Agree
Do not agree or disagree
Disagree
Disagree strongly

Answer

50 I enjoy manual labour.

Agree strongly
Agree
Do not agree or disagree
Disagree
Disagree strongly

Answer

51 I have always been comfortable with being told what to do but often lack the confidence to give orders myself.

Agree strongly
Agree
Do not agree or disagree
Disagree
Disagree strongly

Answer

52 I do not consider it important if someone will not have direct eye contact with me or refuses to shake my hand.

Agree strongly
Agree
Do not agree or disagree
Disagree
Disagree strongly

Answer

53 I hate waiting for something to happen and get bored easily.

Agree strongly
Agree
Do not agree or disagree
Disagree
Disagree strongly

Answer

54 I am not so interested in an easy life but am genuinely interested in helping people.

Agree strongly
Agree
Do not agree or disagree
Disagree
Disagree strongly

Answer

55 On rare occasions it is appropriate to make a racist remark.

Agree strongly
Agree
Do not agree or disagree
Disagree
Disagree strongly

Answer

56 If I have an alcoholic drink in my spare time, it could be something my employer objects to.

Agree strongly
Agree
Do not agree or disagree
Disagree
Disagree strongly

Answer

57 I rarely need to read the operating instructions when I use a piece of equipment for the first time.

Agree strongly
Agree
Do not agree or disagree
Disagree
Disagree strongly

Answer

58   In the role of a firefighter, demonstrating integrity is more important than supporting colleagues.

Agree strongly
Agree
Do not agree or disagree
Disagree
Disagree strongly

Answer

59   I have considerable experience of operating heavy plant and machinery.

Agree strongly
Agree
Do not agree or disagree
Disagree
Disagree strongly

Answer

60   It is not true that women do not make good firefighters.

Agree strongly
Agree
Do not agree or disagree
Disagree
Disagree strongly

Answer

61   I am not the sort of person who gets more done working on my own.

Agree strongly
Agree
Do not agree or disagree
Disagree
Disagree strongly

Answer

62 It is obvious that people should refrain from using bad language at work.

Agree strongly
Agree
Do not agree or disagree
Disagree
Disagree strongly

Answer

63 Because it is the only language they understand, you sometimes have no alternative but to confront aggressive people by being equally aggressive.

Agree strongly
Agree
Do not agree or disagree
Disagree
Disagree strongly

Answer

64 I do not find it difficult to listen to the views of others.

Agree strongly
Agree
Do not agree or disagree
Disagree
Disagree strongly

Answer

65 Success does not belong to the bold.

Agree strongly
Agree
Do not agree or disagree
Disagree
Disagree strongly

Answer

66   It would be wrong to claim that you sometimes have to raise your voice in order to make your point properly.

Agree strongly
Agree
Do not agree or disagree
Disagree
Disagree strongly

Answer

67   It is not OK to use moderately strong language when at work.

Agree strongly
Agree
Do not agree or disagree
Disagree
Disagree strongly

Answer

68   At work there is no need to get involved in a private matter such as a colleague being bullied.

Agree strongly
Agree
Do not agree or disagree
Disagree
Disagree strongly

Answer

69   It is never clever to make a sarcastic remark.

Agree strongly
Agree
Do not agree or disagree
Disagree
Disagree strongly

Answer

70 I sometimes work at heights.

Agree strongly
Agree
Do not agree or disagree
Disagree
Disagree strongly

Answer [   ]

71 I can start a conversation with anyone.

Agree strongly
Agree
Do not agree or disagree
Disagree
Disagree strongly

Answer [   ]

72 It is wrong to withhold information because it is bad news.

Agree strongly
Agree
Do not agree or disagree
Disagree
Disagree strongly

Answer [   ]

73 A problem shared is a problem halved.

Agree strongly
Agree
Do not agree or disagree
Disagree
Disagree strongly

Answer [   ]

74   I like to be doing things and I get restless if I sit around.

Agree strongly
Agree
Do not agree or disagree
Disagree
Disagree strongly

Answer [   ]

75   I have never told a lie in my life.

Agree strongly
Agree
Do not agree or disagree
Disagree
Disagree strongly

Answer [   ]

76   I know the names of my neighbours and speak to them regularly.

Agree strongly
Agree
Do not agree or disagree
Disagree
Disagree strongly

Answer [   ]

77   It would be none of my business if I saw a colleague stealing company property.

Agree strongly
Agree
Do not agree or disagree
Disagree
Disagree strongly

Answer [   ]

78 It is understandable that I prefer to help a colleague who is nice rather than one I find irritating.

Agree strongly
Agree
Do not agree or disagree
Disagree
Disagree strongly

Answer

79 It is human nature to be as lazy as possible whenever possible.

Agree strongly
Agree
Do not agree or disagree
Disagree
Disagree strongly

Answer

80 Some people can't take a joke and they would benefit if they lightened up a bit.

Agree strongly
Agree
Do not agree or disagree
Disagree
Disagree strongly

Answer

81 I am a very active person and I have to keep active.

Agree strongly
Agree
Do not agree or disagree
Disagree
Disagree strongly

Answer

82   Strength is more important to a firefighter than demonstrating commitment.

Agree strongly
Agree
Do not agree or disagree
Disagree
Disagree strongly

Answer

83   An old proverb says that charity begins at home and some argue that it should stop there but I don't agree.

Agree strongly
Agree
Do not agree or disagree
Disagree
Disagree strongly

Answer

84   It would be wrong to lose your temper at work.

Agree strongly
Agree
Do not agree or disagree
Disagree
Disagree strongly

Answer

85   Taking a few pens and some paper home from work for the kids is something lots of people do and it is not really stealing.

Agree strongly
Agree
Do not agree or disagree
Disagree
Disagree strongly

Answer

86   The best sorts of conversations are constructive.

Agree strongly
Agree
Do not agree or disagree
Disagree
Disagree strongly

Answer

87   I sometimes find it hard to control myself.

Agree strongly
Agree
Do not agree or disagree
Disagree
Disagree strongly

Answer

88   Being able to deal sympathetically with people who are distressed is more important to the role of a firefighter than demonstrating a commitment to equal opportunities.

Agree strongly
Agree
Do not agree or disagree
Disagree
Disagree strongly

Answer

89   It is OK to lose one's temper occasionally as long as that does not last long and one does not hold a grudge.

Agree strongly
Agree
Do not agree or disagree
Disagree
Disagree strongly

Answer

90   I go out of my way to encourage and support others.

Agree strongly
Agree
Do not agree or disagree
Disagree
Disagree strongly

Answer [   ]

91   Maintaining local knowledge and community links is a very important aspect of the work of firefighters.

Agree strongly
Agree
Do not agree or disagree
Disagree
Disagree strongly

Answer [   ]

92   If I thought someone was being bullied then I would give the bully some of his or her own medicine.

Agree strongly
Agree
Do not agree or disagree
Disagree
Disagree strongly

Answer [   ]

93   I am motivated by money more than by the desire to serve my community.

Agree strongly
Agree
Do not agree or disagree
Disagree
Disagree strongly

Answer [   ]

94 Firefighting is more important than fire prevention.

Agree strongly
Agree
Do not agree or disagree
Disagree
Disagree strongly

Answer [ ]

95 I am not the sort of person who lets things build up until I blow my top.

Agree strongly
Agree
Do not agree or disagree
Disagree
Disagree strongly

Answer [ ]

96 If I was being bullied then I would report it and expect my line manager to help put a stop to it.

Agree strongly
Agree
Do not agree or disagree
Disagree
Disagree strongly

Answer [ ]

97 Teamwork is fine up to a point but when the going gets really tough then it is every person for themselves.

Agree strongly
Agree
Do not agree or disagree
Disagree
Disagree strongly

Answer [ ]

98   It is better to help a neighbour than a stranger.

Agree strongly
Agree
Do not agree or disagree
Disagree
Disagree strongly

Answer

99   I should not find it annoying if someone asks me to take my shoes off before I enter their house.

Agree strongly
Agree
Do not agree or disagree
Disagree
Disagree strongly

Answer

100   I see no reason not to call a firefighter a fireman.

Agree strongly
Agree
Do not agree or disagree
Disagree
Disagree strongly

Answer

End of questionnaire.

CHAPTER 3

Written tests and practice questions

The recruitment process to become a firefighter includes a set of psychometric tests. After the sift of application forms, these tests represent the next great challenge in your quest to become a firefighter.

It may be that you are required to undertake a physical fitness test on the same day as the written tests. If this is the case, be sure that you are training both mentally and physically in preparation for what will be a very important day. See Chapter 5 for advice on any physical test.

Practice can make the difference between passing and failing in the written tests. This chapter comprises hundreds of practice questions relevant to the tests used by fire authorities to select firefighters. Answers and many explanations are provided in Chapter 6.

If you would like more practice material than is contained in this and the next chapter, then you will find suitable material in the following Kogan Page titles:

Ultimate Psychometric Tests (2nd edition);

The Numeracy Test Workbook (2nd edition);

The Verbal Reasoning Workbook.

The types of written test in use

The written test comprises a series of sub-tests that will be administrated one after the other with a short pause between each. These sub-tests are multiple-choice items where you have to select one answer as correct from a number of suggestions. The structure of some of the previous selection tests required you to listen to a taped message or watch a video and then answer questions against a time limit. These papers do not feature in the new structure but I have included practice for them (Chapter 4) because at the time of going to print a few authorities were still using them.

Expect the speed at which you must work to vary between the sub-tests. You may find that in the first test you have sufficient time to complete the questions and check your answers carefully. But do not assume that this will be the case in all the sub-tests. The next may require you to work very quickly and if you start it with the same careful, thorough approach that you adopted in the first test you may find that you run out of time and are told to stop before you have attempted all the questions.

Take care to attempt all the questions and be sure to read the instructions at the bottom of each page of the test booklet. Each test is made up of a number of pages and at the bottom of each page you will be told to 'turn over the page'. Only when you have reached the end of the sub-test will the instruction read: 'End of test. Do not turn over the page.'

This book provides practice material and advice on the sub-tests currently used by the Fire Service nationally. Remember if you need more material and are having difficulties finding it, or if some of the sub-tests have changed and you cannot find suitable practice material, then e-mail me at help@mikebryon.com detailing the sort of practice question you are seeking and I will be happy to provide you with details.

How practice can help

You must seek to achieve the very best score possible in the written tests. Every point counts, and two things will help you do this. First, appreciate that practice prior to the test will help you to become familiar with the test's demands, build up speed and accuracy, avoid common mistakes and deal with any nervousness. If passing is important to you then you should be prepared to make a major commitment in terms of setting time aside to practise. Second, realize that doing well in a test is not simply down to intelligence but also requires you to be determined to do well and to try very hard. When the test administrator says 'Stop! Please put your pencils down,' you should feel exhausted as a result of the mental effort you have made. Otherwise you risk not doing yourself justice.

Practice will mean the difference between pass and fail for some candidates. However, if you have never got on with maths or if your reading skills are not what they could be, then the practice contained here may not be sufficient. If you have difficulties with your numeracy or literacy and are determined to become a firefighter, then get hold of the recommended further reading and if you still need more practice then consider going along to a college of further education or some other institution and enrolling on a foundation literacy or numeracy course. It really could make all the difference. When you have passed the written test and are invited for interview, don't forget to mention the fact that you were so committed to becoming a firefighter that you went to college to improve yourself. It will be a credit to you.

If you suffer from a learning disability such as dyslexia and have been formally assessed by an educational psychologist, then you may be allowed extra time in which to complete the written test. Contact the fire authority straight away and ask them if they are able to accommodate your disability.

To maximize the benefits of practice you should be prepared to practise for a minimum of 20 hours over the weeks leading up to your test. If you can obtain sufficient material and can commit the time, then practise a lot more than this. But remember that if you are really weak at maths or English you need to be prepared to make a major commitment over months. There are two sorts of practice you need to undertake.

Practice type 1

Work on realistic practice questions from this chapter in a relaxed situation. The aim here is to get used to the style of question, and to realize what skills are being examined and relearn them. If you get questions wrong, go over them and understand why you are getting them wrong. Use this time to recognize what you need to do better in order to improve your performance in the test. Focus most of your time on what you are least good at.

Practice type 2

Once you feel confident in each of the types of question that you face in the real firefighter test, start practising on realistic questions under strict time constraints and under exam-type conditions. You will find realistic practice tests in Chapter 4. The aim of this second sort of practice is to get used to answering questions under the pressure of time and to build up your speed and accuracy in answering questions when under pressure. If you can, get someone to act as a test administrator to read out the instructions, tell you when to begin and stop you when you have run out of time. Help from someone is really essential for practice in any test where you have to listen to a passage and then answer questions.

On the day of the test

To understand what it will be like on the day, think back to the exams at school. You are invited to attend a training or recruitment centre at a particular time – do not be even a minute late, and dress smartly. You are likely to be one of many candidates invited that day. If you are to undertake a physical test as well as the written one, then you will need to bring a change of sports clothes and training shoes, and you may well need to attend the centre for most of the day. All this detail will be included in your letter of invitation, so read it carefully.

It is really important that you listen carefully to the instructions provided before the test begins. You may feel nervous and this may affect your concentration, so make yourself focus on what is being said. Much of what you will be told will be a repeat of the information provided in the test description sent to you with the letter inviting you to the test. So read and re-read this document before the day of the test.

Pay particular attention to instructions detailing how many questions there are in each sub-test, and then during the test make sure that you have answered all the questions. I have seen candidates who have failed to turn over the page during a test and so missed more than half the items. Had they listened to the instructions more carefully then they would have answered all 30 questions rather than reaching the bottom of the page and deciding that the test must be over when they had only answered 10 of them.

It is important to organize your time before the test, and it is even more essential that you keep track of time during the test and manage how long you spend on any one question. You must keep going right up to the end. If possible, take the last few minutes to go over the questions checking your work. This is where the practice at mock exams under strict time limits really helps.

You should aim to get the right balance between speed and accuracy. To do well you must work quickly whilst making the minimum of mistakes.

Everyone gets some answers wrong. It is better that you risk getting some questions wrong but attempt every question rather than double-check every answer and be told that you have run out of time before you have finished all of them.

When you hit a difficult section or question don't lose heart. Just keep going – you may well find that you come next to a section or question in which you can excel.

If you do not know an answer then educated guessing is worthwhile and worth practising. If you are unsure of an answer to a multiple-choice question, consider all the suggested answers and try ruling some out as wrong. This way you can reduce the number of suggested answers from which to guess and hopefully increase your chances of guessing correctly.

Make sure that you adopt the right approach during the test. The candidates who do best are the ones who look forward to the challenge of a test and the opportunity to demonstrate their abilities. They realize that they have nothing to lose if they do their best and 'go for it'. It is critical that you approach the test with confidence in your own abilities, and preparation is the key to confidence.

What to do if you fail

It is likely that over half of the candidates will fail. If you are one of those who do not pass, then understand that it does not mean that you do not have the potential to be a firefighter. Ask the authority to provide you with feedback on your score and identify which part of the test you had a problem with. Recall and note down the types of question and the level of difficulty that they represented. Be honest with yourself and try to assess what it is you need to do in order to pass the next time. I know firefighters who repeatedly failed the written tests. For some of them, it was only when they set about a major programme of improving their maths or English or both that they then went on to pass. Others simply needed to get more used to the test and working under the pressure of time in an exam.

To re-apply you will have to wait for another recruitment round and you may have to submit another application form, and assuming that you pass the application form sift, you will be called again for the test. In some cases you will only have to resit the paper you failed. In the meantime plan a programme of revision and improvement and work hard on the areas in which you were weakest last time. Do not forget to maintain your programme of physical fitness training at the same time.

It will take courage and determination to try again and to keep working to improve yourself until you pass. But courage and determination are exactly the qualities that a firefighter is expected to demonstrate. So decide whether you are prepared to make the necessary commitment and, if you are and you go on to succeed, then it will be something of which you can be rightly proud.

Practice questions

In the remainder of this chapter you will find hundreds of practice questions relevant to the firefighter practice test. Some of the questions are intended to help you to develop the skills required in the real test. These questions may therefore be easier than the real ones and in a different format, but for some candidates they are essential preparation and will help you to achieve the confidence and speed demanded by the real test. Realistic practice tests are provided in Chapter 4.

Understanding information

In this type of test, your task is to read a passage and answer a series of questions. Each question comprises a statement about the passage and you must indicate which of the suggested answers is correct. You make your decision based only on the information contained in the passage.

This sort of question may seem straightforward, in that you can always refer back to the passage to answer each question. However, the tests are done under tight time constraints and such an approach may mean that you run out of time before you have attempted all the questions. The best approach requires just one fast, very attentive reading of the passage before answering the questions, perhaps going back to the passage but on only a few occasions.

It is really important that you do not bring to the question knowledge or information not contained in the passage. You should resist answering the question on the basis of any information other than that contained in the passage even if it is on a subject of which you know a great deal.

For example, suppose the passage says 'Pigs can fly' and the question asks 'Can pigs fly?' Even though we all know pigs cannot, the correct answer is that pigs can fly. Equally, if the passage makes no reference to whether or not pigs can fly then the answer to the question would be 'Cannot say'.

Please note two things about this practice. First you will find that the passages relating to the initial 50 practice questions are all on subjects related to the Fire Service; however, they should not be relied on as a source of information on the subject of fire prevention or firefighting, nor do they necessarily describe correctly how you should act in any of the situations described. Second, note that the questions ask you to carry out a task that is different from the real firefighter understanding-information test. These questions require you to say whether a statement is true or false or if it is impossible to establish whether it is true or false. In the real test you must select an answer from a list of suggestions. This difference is intentional. The 'true, false, cannot say' style of question is a really effective way to get better at all types of understanding-information tests. The questions will ensure that you become confident in interpreting passages and recognize the typical traps and tricks. Later on in the chapter I provide questions in the style found in the real tests.

With practice you can improve your performance in this kind of test. Try the following 50 questions, which are all on subjects related to the Fire Service, and seek to build up your speed and confidence. Answers and many explanations are provided in Chapter 6. You will find a further 50 practice questions, making 100 in total, further on.

The first 50 practice questions

Important note

Please note that the passages are made up for the purpose of providing realistic practice only and in many respects may be factually incorrect. The passages should not be relied on as a source of information on the subject of fire prevention or firefighting, nor do they necessarily describe correctly how you should act in any of the situations described.

Passage 1

Dressed in a firefighter's protective suit, boots and helmet and holding no more than a fire blanket, I entered the blackened room to face a flaming pan on a cooker. The heat and smoke were increasing by the second. I guarded my hands with the blanket and held it up high, remembering my training that the blanket had to be above the flames and should never be thrown. I advanced carefully, slowly, to avoid a slip or trip that could prove fatal. I draped the blanket over the blazing chip pan. Immediately the blanket was sucked into the container by the flames creating a vacuum as they fought for oxygen, and the fire was out.

I had attended a day of theory in fire prevention and firefighting at the Maritime Safety Centre in Gosport. I learnt that a fire aboard a ship was most likely to happen because of poorly maintained electrical equipment and oil or grease left to accumulate around hot engines. On the second day of the course we put into practice what we had been taught.

Questions

Q1 The trainee firefighter was wearing everyday street clothes.

True

False

Cannot say

Answer ┌─────────────┐
         │   │
         └─────────────┘

Q2 The fire was aboard a ship.

True
False
Cannot say

Answer

Q3 The thing on fire was a chip pan.

True
False
Cannot say

Answer

Q4 The fire blanket was sucked into the pan before the flames died.

True
False
Cannot say

Answer

Q5 The training centre was in Southampton.

True
False
Cannot say

Answer

Q6 Oil and grease cause most fires on ships.

True
False
Cannot say

Answer

Q7   The course covered both firefighting and fire prevention.

True
False
Cannot say

Answer [   ]

Q8   Chip pans should not be used on board a boat.

True
False
Cannot say

Answer [   ]

Q9   The trainee was taught to walk slowly to avoid tripping.

True
False
Cannot say

Answer [   ]

Q10   You have to be physically and mentally fit to fight a fire.

True
False
Cannot say

Answer [   ]

Passage 2

Holding a cup of water fixed to a very long pole, the instructor carefully poured the water into the relit pan of burning oil, which by this stage was very hot. Suddenly, there was an explosion and a ball of flames hit the roof of the room and rapidly rolled out across the whole room. The speed and intensity of the reaction was shocking and frightening. The instructor had deliberately made the potentially lethal error of trying to put out a class B fire (a burning liquid) with water. We had been told that the flame could move at 5 metres per second and was fuelled by droplets of burning oil carried by steam.

Another fire risk on ships is aerosol cans, which are used to hold substances such as furniture polish, kitchen cleaner, fly killer, oil and so on. On a boat there are often many of these cans and if a fire occurs and one of these cans is consumed by the flames then there is a high risk that an explosion will occur.

Before the end of the second day of the course the instructor demonstrated the use of foam, carbon dioxide and dry powder extinguishers, and ensured that each trainee had first-hand experience of each type. It was explained that the carbon dioxide extinguishers were pressurized vessels and so the heaviest, and that dry powder when set off created a great deal of white dust.

Questions

Q11   You are unlikely to find many aerosols on boats.

True

False

Cannot say

Answer ☐

Q12   The trainee firefighters practised with a CO_2 and foam-filled extinguisher only.

True

False

Cannot say

Answer ☐

Q13   The explosion happened because water was poured on to a burning liquid.

True

False

Cannot say

Answer ☐

Q14 The passage states that the trainees witnessed two explosions.

True
False
Cannot say

Answer [   ]

Q15 The heaviest extinguishers are pressure vessels.

True
False
Cannot say

Answer [   ]

Q16 In the passage the trainees were warned that it is the smoke that kills you and not the flames.

True
False
Cannot say

Answer [   ]

Q17 The two-day course covered both the theory and practice of fire prevention.

True
False
Cannot say

Answer [   ]

Q18 A class B fire can be put out with a foam-filled extinguisher.

True
False
Cannot say

Answer [   ]

Q19 In seven seconds the ball of flame caused by the burning oil exploding could travel further than 25 metres.

True

False

Cannot say

Answer _____

Q20 Foam extinguishers give off a white dust.

True

False

Cannot say

Answer _____

Passage 3

Under recent legislation every place of work should have a written fire emergency plan. It should be specific to the workplace and detail the procedure in place in the event of fire. The plan should comment on the action to be taken on the discovery of a fire, how staff are to warn others of the emergency, how the fire brigade are to be informed and how staff are to evacuate the building and where to assemble. The firefighting equipment provided must be identified and properly maintained. The plan should be regularly practised by all the staff involved and the alarm system tested weekly to ensure that it is functioning properly.

Questions

Q21 A fire emergency plan should detail actions to be taken on the discovery of a fire.

True

False

Cannot say

Answer _____

Q22   The passage states that firefighting equipment must be properly maintained.

True
False
Cannot say

Answer [   ]

Q23   The plan is to specify the procedure in the event of a fire.

True
False
Cannot say

Answer [   ]

Q24   The passage states that an alarm system must be fitted.

True
False
Cannot say

Answer [   ]

Q25   The point of this passage is to explain how to tackle an electrical fire at work.

True
False
Cannot say

Answer [   ]

Passage 4

Firefighting always comes second to the safety of yourself and others. The first action on discovering a fire should be to raise the alarm. This may mean shouting 'Fire, fire!' followed by the operation of a fire alarm call point if there is one. Once the alarm has been raised, circumstances will determine whether or not you should try to fight the fire. However, more important than fighting a fire is ensuring the evacuation of people. It is important to make sure that people do not use lifts or go back into a building. People should only attempt to fight a fire if they are trained to do so and it does not involve unacceptable risk.

Questions

Q26   Once you have raised the alarm the most important thing is to evacuate the people.

True
False
Cannot say

Answer

Q27   Disabled people should use the lifts in order that they may leave the building quickly.

True
False
Cannot say

Answer

Q28   People once evacuated should assemble at the designated locations.

True
False
Cannot say

Answer

Q29   The passage states that a fire warden should raise the alarm by shouting 'Fire, fire!'

True
False
Cannot say

Answer

Q30   Firefighting is something you should consider after completing all the other tasks.

True
False
Cannot say

Answer [   ]

Passage 5

All workplaces should be provided with adequate equipment for fighting fires. However, only people trained in its use should attempt to operate it. When deciding which type of extinguisher to use it is important to take into account the type of fire involved. Before anyone starts to fight a fire they must make sure that they have a clear exit route. When tackling the fire they should always position themselves between the fire and the way out.

Water is used on class A fires, which include solid materials. Foam can be used on type B and C fires, which include fires that involve liquids (type B) and gases (type C). Carbon dioxide can be used on electrical fires. Dry powder can be used on most types of fire.

Questions

Q31   When fighting a fire your back will most likely be facing your exit.

True
False
Cannot say

Answer [   ]

Q32   A burning table would be an example of a class A fire.

True
False
Cannot say

Answer [   ]

Q33 A burning pan of oil could be extinguished with a foam-filled extinguisher.

True

False

Cannot say

Answer [   ]

Q34 The passage states that all homes should be provided with adequate firefighting equipment.

True

False

Cannot say

Answer [   ]

Q35 This passage explains the advantages of each type of extinguisher.

True

False

Cannot say

Answer [   ]

Passage 6

The greatest danger is the spread of fire, heat and smoke. If this happens, the main risk to people is from the smoke, which can quickly overcome them and prevent them from escaping. If there is no adequate means of escape or if a fire can become big before it is noticed, then people may become trapped or overcome by heat or smoke before they can evacuate. An assessment of the risk of fire should include the likely speed of growth and spread of any fire and the heat and smoke generated. It should also estimate the number of people that may be found in an area and describe how they are to become aware of a fire and how they will make their escape.

Questions

Q36 How quickly a fire might spread should be considered in an assessment of the risk of fire.

True
False
Cannot say

Answer ☐

Q37 The passage states that if people become trapped then smoke and heat are the main threats as they can incapacitate them.

True
False
Cannot say

Answer ☐

Q38 Firefighting equipment and full training in its operation must be provided.

True
False
Cannot say

Answer ☐

Q39 A smoke alarm would quickly raise the alarm in the event of a fire.

True
False
Cannot say

Answer ☐

Q40   A workplace assessment should investigate how workers are to become aware of a fire.

True
False
Cannot say

Answer [   ]

Passage 7

For fire to occur there must be a source of ignition, fuel and oxygen. If all three are present then the risk of fire exists; if they are in close proximity then the risk of fire increases. Oxygen is present in the air; sometimes it is also present in chemical form. Ignition can come from naked flames, hot surfaces, friction caused by drive belts, electrical sparks from static electricity or switches. Fuel can be anything that burns, including textiles, wood, paper, plastics or furniture. Liquids, including petrol, paints and adhesives, and gases such as acetylene are also potential fuels.

A risk assessment should list the potential sources of ignition and fuels that are present and describe how a fire can be prevented.

Questions

Q41   The passage states that if a source of ignition, fuel and oxygen are all present then a fire will occur.

True
False
Cannot say

Answer [   ]

Q42   Oxygen is found only in the air.

True
False
Cannot say

Answer [   ]

Q43   The closer together a source of ignition, fuel and oxygen are, the greater the risk of a fire.

True
False
Cannot say

Answer [   ]

Q44   Acetylene is more inflammable than petrol.

True
False
Cannot say

Answer [   ]

Q45   This passage describes the conditions necessary for a fire to occur.

True
False
Cannot say

Answer [   ]

Passage 8

A fire risk assessment seeks to identify the risk of a fire occurring and the fire hazards that are present. A hazard is something that could cause harm, while risk is the chance of that hazard actually causing harm.

An assessment must be specific to a particular place and must be carried out by someone who understands basic fire-safety principles and has knowledge about the particular place. A risk assessment should identify all the fire hazards and risks present in a location and then determine whether or not they are acceptable and whether further action is required to reduce the risk.

Questions

Q46   An assessment must be written by someone who knows the place to which an assessment relates.

True

False

Cannot say

Answer

Q47   If an assessment identifies unacceptable fire hazards then it should determine whether further action should be taken in order to reduce those hazards.

True

False

Cannot say

Answer

Q48   The passage makes it clear that a naked flame and petrol represent a fire hazard.

True

False

Cannot say

Answer

Q49   Once the fire hazards and risks are identified, then an assessment is complete.

True

False

Cannot say

Answer

Q50   The passage describes features of a fire risk assessment.

True

False

Cannot say

Answer

Another *50* understanding-information questions

In this section you will find another 50 practice questions, and again you must read a number of passages and answer the questions referring to those passages.

The difference with these practice questions is that the subjects of the passages are not issues about fire prevention but instead describe some of the UK's communities and issues relevant to them. Use the information to improve your understanding of these communities while practising for this important test. Note that from question 30 onwards, instead of answering 'true', 'false' or 'cannot say' you must choose which of four suggested answers is the correct one. In the real test, this is the style that the questions will follow.

Passage 1

Different people mean different things when they speak of antisocial behaviour. It lacks an agreed definition and covers a very wide range of activities, some of which are quite minor and others very serious. Complaints relating to minor transgressions, for example noisy neighbours or an untidy garden, can be taken to a local housing office but they will only help if both the complainant and alleged perpetrator are their tenants, or in other words are resident in their properties. If the local housing office will not help then complaints can be taken to a local mediation service, a private landlord (if their tenant is involved) or a firm of solicitors. The police deal only with cases of severe antisocial behaviour, for example drug dealing, racial harassment and domestic violence.

Questions

Q1 The passage states that children causing problems in a neigh-bourhood can be considered to be behaving in an antisocial manner.

True
False
Cannot say

Answer [   ]

Q2 If you have a complaint of antisocial behaviour against a tenant of a local housing office but you are not a tenant your-self, then you can take your complaint to a local mediation service.

True
False
Cannot say

Answer [   ]

Q3 There is no commonly held definition of the term 'antisocial behaviour'.

True
False
Cannot say

Answer [   ]

Q4 If you and the perpetrator are residents of properties man-aged by a housing office then you could take a complaint of racial harassment to them.

True
False
Cannot say

Answer [   ]

Q5   The police will deal with a complaint about an untidy garden but only if neither the complainant nor the perpetrator are residents of properties managed by a local housing office.

True

False

Cannot say

Answer [   ]

Passage 2

Almost everyone who does voluntary work has a positive opinion of their community. They enjoy living in their area and believe that people there are willing to help each other. They trust the people within their community and feel that people there share the same values as themselves. Contrast this with the views of people who do not undertake any voluntary work. They do not enjoy living in their area as much and feel that people are not very inclined to help each other.

Questions

Q6   The author of the passage would agree with the statement that people who don't do voluntary work are likely to have a less positive view of their community than people who do.

True

False

Cannot say

Answer [   ]

Q7   The passage states that people who don't do voluntary work feel that they share the same values as other people in their community.

True

False

Cannot say

Answer [   ]

Q8   The passage states that people who do no voluntary work do
not enjoy living in their area.

True
False
Cannot say

Answer [   ]

Q9   People who do no voluntary work do not trust other people in
their community as much as people who do voluntary work.

True
False
Cannot say

Answer [   ]

Q10   Not everyone who does voluntary work has a positive opinion of their community.

True
False
Cannot say

Answer [   ]

Passage 3

A Credit Union is both a sort of club and a bank. Members can save
money, and be paid a good rate of interest, or they can borrow at
a low rate of interest. Credit Unions are able to pay good rates of
interest to their savers and charge borrowers low rates because they
are cooperatives that are owned and managed by the members on
a not-for-profit basis. They have been set up all over the country and
are growing fast. The average membership is about 3,500 and
typically they have lent a total of £800,000. Credit Unions also save
money because they do not have to maintain a chain of high-street
outlets but instead members deposit savings and make payments
at post offices, convenience stores and over the internet.

Questions

Q11   Credit Unions offer low-interest loans.

True
False
Cannot say

Answer [   ]

Q12   You can't draw your savings from a Credit Union account from a cashpoint machine.

True
False
Cannot say

Answer [   ]

Q13   Anyone can have a savings account with a Credit Union.

True
False
Cannot say

Answer [   ]

Q14   A Credit Union with 2,000 members would be considered large.

True
False
Cannot say

Answer [   ]

Q15   Credit Unions pay higher rates of interest on their saving accounts and charge borrowers lower rates of interest than the rates charged by high-street banks.

True
False
Cannot say

Answer [   ]

Passage 4

Community involvement includes anything from helping a neighbour to undertaking some voluntary work for a local organization, raising funds for a local youth club or nursing home, or becoming a school governor or local councillor. People start to get involved in their local community for a number of reasons. The most common is having a new family: becoming a parent can change people's priorities and make them more interested in local facilities such as schools that they may want to improve. Being new to an area is another reason; people are keen to get involved so that they can make friends in the community. Sometimes a tragedy that affects local people makes individuals want to become more active in the community, stimulating them to come together in an attempt to improve things or make sure that such a thing will not happen again.

Questions

Q16   The second most common reason why people get involved in their community is that they are new to the area.

True
False
Cannot say

Answer   [   ]

Q17   The reasons given for people becoming involved in their community are all good.

True
False
Cannot say

Answer   [   ]

Q18 A reason people become more involved in the community is that they decide to stay in an area, so they decide 'this is now my home' and it becomes more worthwhile helping to make that area better.

True
False
Cannot say

Answer [   ]

Q19 The passage states that an example of community involvement includes raising money for a local charity.

True
False
Cannot say

Answer [   ]

Q20 All the reasons given for greater community involvement are motivations to become involved in the local community rather than involvement outside the local area.

True
False
Cannot say

Answer [   ]

Passage 5

Social exclusion occurs when people have no access to things that the majority of the population enjoys. We might say that people are socially excluded if they are, for example, unemployed, on a low income, discriminated against or lack key skills. Social exclusion is particularly harmful when whole communities are affected. It is also very harmful and unfortunately common for people to suffer more than one of the causes of social exclusion. For example, someone who is unemployed is very likely to also be on a low income and more likely to live in poor-quality housing and suffer from ill health. Any one of these issues is hard to overcome but when an individual faces a series of such problems, then they combine to make it almost impossible for that person to break out from the cycle of deprivation and exclusion.

Questions

Q21 Social exclusion is something that only affects individuals.

True

False

Cannot say

Answer _____

Q22 The author of the passage would agree that someone who suffers one of the causes of social exclusion is likely to suffer from some of the other causes too.

True

False

Cannot say

Answer _____

Q23 In a wealthy society people do not suffer from social exclusion.

True

False

Cannot say

Answer _____

Q24 It is reasonable to infer from the passage that someone unable to read or write may be socially excluded.

True

False

Cannot say

Answer _____

Q25 The passage states that there is no solution to social exclusion.

True
False
Cannot say

Answer

Passage 6

The 2001 UK Census shows a 9 per cent decline to just under 400,000 in the total population of the city of Manchester. The city has a high number of students studying at the two universities and the second-largest Jewish population in the UK. It also has one of the largest Muslim populations in Britain and many people from Manchester have Irish ancestry. In the Census returns, 80 per cent identified themselves as White British, 9 per cent as Asian or Asian British, 6 per cent as Black or Black British, 3 per cent as mixed race and 2 per cent as Chinese or another ethnic group. When you first look at the figures it seems that Manchester has a very high number of unemployed people, but this conclusion is misleading because the high student population distorts the data.

Questions

Q26 Manchester's black and minority ethnic populations amount to 20 per cent of the population.

True
False
Cannot say

Answer

Q27   The passage states that many people who live in Manchester describe themselves as Irish.

True
False
Cannot say

Answer [   ]

Q28   The Jewish population is the second-largest religious community in Manchester.

True
False
Cannot say

Answer [   ]

Q29   The population of Manchester has fallen.

True
False
Cannot say

Answer [   ]

Q30   It is fair to conclude that Manchester is religiously diverse.

True
False
Cannot say

Answer [   ]

Passage 7

Something like 250,000 Gypsy and Irish Travellers live in the UK, and historically had a nomadic way of life going back far into antiquity. Nowadays perhaps 90 per cent of Gypsies live in houses rather than caravans, but their culture remains with them and many will still travel for some months each year. Many travellers work in trades that they can continue when on the move. Nowadays they work as seasonal agricultural labourers, landscape gardeners, motor trade workers, scrap metal dealers and tree fellers. The life of a traveller remains a difficult one. Gypsies and Irish Travellers suffer from a high incidence of ill health and have life expectancies below the national average. Their children attend school less than children from other ethnic groups, and a sizable minority fail to complete their education or gain qualifications.

Questions

Q31   From a reading of the passage it is true that:

A.   The vast majority of Gypsy and Irish Travellers no longer live in caravans.

B.   Gypsy and Irish Travellers prefer to live in caravans.

C.   Gypsy and Irish Travellers no longer live in caravans.

D.   A large percentage of Gypsy and Irish Travellers still live in caravans.

Answer

Q32   The term 'Gypsy':

A.   Is thought to be derived from 'Egyptian', as people thought Gypsies originated from Egypt.

B.   Is the name of a group of people with a nomadic way of life.

C.   Is the name of a group of people who historically had a nomadic way of life.

D.   Is heard relatively rarely nowadays.

Answer

Q33   The author of the passage would disagree with the statement that:

A.   Many travellers will still travel some months a year.

B.   Travellers don't work.

C.   Travellers suffer from a high incidence of ill health.

D.   Travellers work hard.

Answer

Q34 The culture of Gypsies and Irish Travellers originated:

    A. In the very distant past.

    B. In the last century.

    C. Quite a while ago.

    D. Relatively recently.

Answer _____

Q35 Most children of Gypsies and Irish Travellers:

    A. Pass some exams.

    B. Fail some exams.

    C. Complete their education.

    D. Fail to complete their education.

Answer _____

Passage 8

Long-established communities born and educated in the UK are unlikely to have any practical difficulty in understanding the language in which services are publicized and delivered. However, newer arrivals and newer communities might find language a barrier. Recently the number of languages spoken in the UK has increased because many people have arrived speaking, for example, Polish, Arabic, Swahili and Slovakian. Disabled customers might also find it very difficult to understand or to be understood. To make sure services are used by everyone, an interpreter or translator is sometimes necessary. A translator works with written material while an interpreter works directly with people, interpreting what they say. Technical aids such as audiotapes and induction loops can also help, and providing publications in large print and in Braille is important. Providing translation and technical aids and the services of an interpreter helps ensure genuine equality of opportunity in the delivery of services and makes it clear to minority communities that the service provider is serious about addressing their needs.

Questions

Q36   The passage is about:

A.   Translation.

B.   Good communication.

C.   Poor communication and its role in service delivery.

D.   Good practice in the promotion and delivery of services.

Answer [   ]

Q37   The job of a translator is to:

A.   Meet people and translate what they say.

B.   Translate written work.

C.   Meet people and interpret what they say.

D.   Translate what people say.

Answer [   ]

Q38   You need only to provide the services of an interpreter to members of communities who:

A.   Are new to the UK and do not speak English.

B.   Do not speak good English.

C.   Might find language a barrier.

D.   Are new to the UK, because they have not had time to learn English.

Answer [   ]

Q39   Technology has a role to play in providing:

A.   Value for money.

B.   Equal access to services.

C.   Genuine services.

D.   None of the above.

Answer [   ]

Q40 The number of languages spoken in the UK:

    A. Has recently increased.

    B. Has increased in recent years.

    C. Has dramatically increased.

    D. Will continue to increase.

Answer [   ]

Passage 9

A practical example of equal opportunities at work is a transparent and fair set of written procedures that will help positively resolve any instance of unfair discrimination. Within the first two months of starting work your employer should provide you with written details of your terms of employment, and these should include details of a procedure for disciplinary action and dealing with any grievance you may have.

Should you at some point in your employment have a grievance and be unable to resolve it informally, then you should write to your employer detailing your grievance. Your employer should then arrange a meeting to discuss your grievance and afterwards tell you what they have decided to do to resolve it. If you are not satisfied with the proposal then you have a right to appeal and another meeting should then be arranged. If you are still not satisfied after the second meeting you have the option of taking your grievance to an employment tribunal.

Questions

Q41 It is stated in the passage that:

    A. You are unable to take up a grievance once you have left a job.

    B. Everyone has the option of taking a grievance to an employment tribunal.

    C. You are unable to resolve a grievance informally.

    D. You should write to your employer if you are unable to resolve a grievance informally.

Answer [   ]

Q42 You are:

    A. Allowed to appeal if you are not satisfied after the first meeting.

    B. Not allowed to take someone along to the meetings.

    C. Allowed to take someone along with you to the meetings.

    D. Able to attend two meetings in total.

Answer

Q43 At work if you feel you have been unfairly discriminated against and you cannot resolve it by informal means, then you should:

    A. First use the grievance procedure to try to resolve the matter.

    B. Initially ask for a meeting to discuss your grievance.

    C. At the earliest opportunity take disciplinary action.

    D. Immediately take your grievance to an employment tribunal.

Answer

Q44 In the passage the term 'transparent' is used to mean:

    A. See through.

    B. An operation.

    C. Easily understood.

    D. Obscure.

Answer

Q45 'Informally' in the context of the passage does not mean:

    A. Raising the matter without using the official grievance procedure.

    B. Without authorization.

    C. Talking to your employer about how you feel.

    D. First trying to resolve your grievance in an unofficial way.

Answer

Passage 10

Research has found that people who say they have friends drawn from a mixture of racial groups said that there was less racial prejudice now than five years ago. The study also found that people who agreed with the statement that their community pulled together also felt there was less racial tension today than previously. These findings led the researchers to conclude that how people perceived their neighbourhood, and what sort of friends they had, was suggestive of how prevalent they felt racial prejudice was.

Questions

Q46 The passage reports that the research found that:

A. Racial tension had increased over the last five years.

B. People who answer certain questions in one way are more likely to believe that racial tension had increased.

C. Racial tension had decreased over the last five years.

D. People who answer certain questions in one way are more likely to believe that racial tension had decreased.

Answer [   ]

Q47 The research suggests that people who felt racial prejudice was less prevalent now than five years ago might also agree with the statement that:

A. They have friends of different racial groups than their own.

B. Racial prejudice was widespread.

C. Racial prejudice was rare.

D. Racial prejudice was out of order.

Answer [   ]

Q48   The research found that:

A.   Racial tension had decreased over the last five years.

B.   People agreed with the statement that their community pulled together.

C.   People who agreed with the statement that their community pulled together felt there was less racial tension today than previously.

D.   Racial tension had increased over the last five years.

Answer [   ]

Q49   Another word or phrase for 'community' is:

A.   Pulling together.

B.   Neighbourhood.

C.   Racial tension.

D.   Friends.

Answer [   ]

Q50   You:

A.   Can infer from the passage that people who felt that their communities pulled together live in communities that suffer less racial tension.

B.   Can infer from the passage that people who felt that their communities pulled together live in communities in which large ethnic minority groups also live.

C.   Can infer from the passage that people who felt that their communities pulled together also had friends who belong to a racial group different to their own.

D.   Can't infer from the passage that people who felt that their communities pulled together also had friends who belong to a racial group different to their own.

Answer [   ]

Get super-numerate

Revise the basics

Practise to become fast, accurate and confident in the key mathe-matical operations of addition, subtraction, multiplication and simple division and percentages. If you are sure that you already are, then feel free to miss this section.

Make sure that you get 100 per cent of these sums right working really quickly. So many tests require these skills that you must attend on the day able to do them almost without thinking. That will allow you to concentrate on the other components of the questions.

If you need more practice then you will find it in the titles recom-mended on page 66. You might also get someone to help you and make up lots more examples.

There are a number of methods that you can use to answer these questions. Stick to the ones you know or that your helper explains to you. For this reason I have not provided explanations to these questions.

Attempt all these questions without using a calculator. See how close you can get to answering the 30 examples in 2 minutes 30 seconds (5 seconds a question!). If you can't work that quickly then you need to practise more. You will find hundreds more practice questions in the Kogan Page title *The Numeracy Test Workbook*.

Addition

Q1 $5 + 5 =$

Q2 $7 + 8 =$

Q3 $6 + 7 =$

Q4 $7 + 5 =$

Q5 $6 + 8 =$

Q6 $5 + 8 =$

Q7 $3 + 9 =$

Q8 $4 + 6 =$

Q9 $9 + 4 =$

Q10 $2 + 9 =$

Q11 $12 + 11 =$

Q12 $14 + 13 =$

Q13 $15 + 16 =$

Q14 $14 + 11 =$

Q15 $16 + 17 =$

Q16 $15 + 15 =$

Q17 $18 + 14 =$

Q18 $19 + 17 =$

Q19 $13 + 18 =$

Q20 $19 + 20 =$

Q21 $326 + 363 =$

Q22 $542 + 317 =$

Q23 $749 + 250 =$

Q24 $273 + 361 =$

Q25 $824 + 107 =$

Q26 $375 + 497 =$

Q27 $462 + 498 =$

Q28 $800 + 693 =$

Q29 $673 + 469 =$

Q30 $927 + 784 =$

Sums that relate to the calculation of time

Practise to be quick in working with the units hours and minutes; give all answers in hours and minutes.

Q31   45 minutes + 12 minutes =

Q32   34 minutes + 1 hour 20 minutes =

Q33   19 minutes + 25 minutes =

Q34   17 minutes + 1 hour 38 minutes =

Q35   09 minutes + 1 hour 11 minutes =

Q36   1 hour 27 minutes + 19 minutes =

Q37   15 minutes + 45 minutes =

Q38   1 hour 16 minutes + 23 minutes =

Q39   1 hour 04 minutes + 1 hour 52 minutes =

Q40   1 hour 47 minutes + 56 minutes =

Q41   39 minutes + 1 hour 47 minutes =

Q42   1 hour 25 minutes + 1 hour 38 minutes =

Q43   1 hour 15 minutes + 1 hour 56 minutes =

Q44   55 minutes + 3 hours 55 minutes =

Q45   17 minutes + 7 hours 7 minutes =

Q46   3 hours 59 minutes + 1 hour 29 minutes =

Q47   5 hours and 17 minutes + 5 hours and 42 minutes =

Q48   2 hours 15 minutes + 4 hours 45 minutes =

Q49   4 hours 12 minutes + 7 hours 55 minutes =

Q50   3 hours 27 minutes + 5 hours 45 minutes =

Subtraction

Attempt all these questions without using a calculator. See how close you can get to answering the 30 examples in 2 minutes 30 seconds (5 seconds a question!).

Q1 $12 - 11 =$

Q2 $14 - 8 =$

Q3 $16 - 9 =$

Q4 $15 - 7 =$

Q5 $23 - 17 =$

Q6 $27 - 19 =$

Q7 $29 - 21 =$

Q8 $31 - 19 =$

Q9 $35 - 26 =$

Q10 $42 - 29 =$

Q11 $324 - 211 =$

Q12 $465 - 305 =$

Q13 $864 - 623 =$

Q14 $999 - 308 =$

Q15 $739 - 526 =$

Q16 $358 - 209 =$

Q17 $421 - 271 =$

Q18 $734 - 198 =$

Q19 $402 - 311 =$

Q20 $605 - 418 =$

Q21 $228 - 179 =$

Q22 452 – 177 =

Q23 732 – 483 =

Q24 507 – 312 =

Q25 921 – 553 =

Q26 801 – 364 =

Q27 624 – 289 =

Q28 500 – 362 =

Q29 801 – 387 =

Q30 1,000 – 911 =

More sums that relate to the calculation of time

Practise to be quick in working with the units hours and minutes. Do not use a calculator, and practise until you are completely familiar with this type of question. Work quickly.

Q1 45 minutes – 17 minutes =

Q2 33 minutes – 19 minutes =

Q3 52 minutes – 45 minutes =

Q4 31 minutes – 18 minutes =

Q5 1 hour 12 minutes – 1 hour 06 minutes =

Q6 1 hour 33 minutes – 20 minutes =

Q7 1 hour 03 minutes – 15 minutes =

Q8 1 hour 24 minutes – 33 minutes =

Q9 1 hour 41 minutes – 1 hour 03 minutes =

Q10 1 hour 30 minutes – 57 minutes =

Q11 2 hours 19 minutes – 1 hour 41 minutes =

Q12 2 hours 36 minutes – 1 hour 14 minutes =

Q13 2 hours 09 minutes – 1 hour 16 minutes =

Q14 1 hour 51 minutes – 1 hour 37 minutes =

Q15 2 hours 24 minutes – 1 hour 29 minutes =

Q16 2 hours 12 minutes – 1 hour 47 minutes =

Q17 5 hours 03 minutes – 1 hour 49 minutes =

Q18 4 hours 18 minutes – 3 hours 53 minutes =

Q19 5 hours 21 minutes – 1 hour 47 minutes =

Q20 3 hours 10 minutes – 3 hours 6 minutes =

Q21 4 hours 18 minutes – 1 hour 07 minutes =

Multiplication

Revise your multiplication tables, if you cannot get these examples right very quickly.

Attempt all these questions without using a calculator. See how close you can get to answering each question in five seconds!

Q1 $5 \times 6 =$

Q2 $6 \times 3 =$

Q3 $8 \times 4 =$

Q4 $9 \times 2 =$

Q5 $6 \times 6 =$

Q6 $2 \times 8 =$

Q7 $7 \times 3 =$

Q8 $7 \times 5 =$

Q9 $3 \times 9 =$

Q10 $6 \times 8 =$

Q11 $4 \times 8 =$

Q12 $9 \times 4 =$

Q13 $5 \times 11 =$

Q14 $7 \times 6 =$

Q15 $7 \times 7 =$

Q16 $8 \times 7 =$

Q17 $6 \times 9 =$

Q18 $7 \times 9 =$

Q19 $8 \times 9 =$

Q20 $11 \times 8 =$

Still more sums that relate to the calculation of time

Get really well practised in the calculation of time. It will stand you in very good stead for the questions in the real firefighter written test. Express your answers to the following questions in hours and minutes. For example, 125 minutes = 2 hours and 5 minutes.

Use scrap paper to do your workings out, but do not use a calculator.

To help you do these questions quickly, memorize the following:

1 hour   = 60 minutes
2 hours = 120 minutes
3 hours = 180 minutes
4 hours = 240 minutes
5 hours = 300 minutes
6 hours = 360 minutes
7 hours = 420 minutes
8 hours = 480 minutes
9 hours = 540 minutes

Now attempt these questions:

Q1   What is 20 minutes multiplied by 8?

Answer [   ]

Q2   What is 4 minutes multiplied by 18?

Answer [   ]

Q3   What is 55 minutes multiplied by 3?

Answer [   ]

Q4   How long is 30 minutes multiplied by 17?

Answer [   ]

Q5   What is 7 minutes multiplied by 11?

Answer [   ]

Q6   What is 22 minutes multiplied by 9?

Answer [   ]

Q7   How long is 90 minutes multiplied by 6?

Answer [   ]

Q8   What is 24 minutes multiplied by 5?

Answer [   ]

Q9   What is 12 minutes multiplied by 8?

Answer [   ]

Q10 How long is 20 minutes multiplied by 12?

Answer [   ]

Q11 What is 45 minutes multiplied by 6?

Answer [   ]

Q12   How long is 3 minutes multiplied by 50?

Answer [   ]

Q13   How long is 54 minutes multiplied by 5?

Answer [   ]

Q14   What is 8 minutes multiplied by 15?

Answer [   ]

Q15   How long is 18 minutes multiplied by 10?

Answer [   ]

Q16   How long is 57 minutes multiplied by 10?

Answer [   ]

Q17   What is 18 minutes multiplied by 6?

Answer [   ]

Q18   How long is 10 minutes multiplied by 33?

Answer [   ]

Q19   What is 24 minutes multiplied by 4?

Answer [   ]

Q20   How long is 120 minutes multiplied by 3?

Answer [   ]

Division and percentages

Attempt all these questions without using a calculator. Work as quickly as possible; if you are slow at division then you need to practise your multiplication tables some more. Revise the rules and undertake more practice if there are any questions you cannot do.

Q1 $12 \div 3 =$

Q2 $25 \div 2 =$

Q3 $28 \div 4 =$

Q4 $36 \div 4 =$

Q5 $72 \div 8 =$

Q6 $55 \div 11 =$

Q7 $54 \div 18 =$

Q8 $81 \div 9 =$

Q9 $240 \div 20 =$

Q10 $270 \div 30 =$

Q11 $85 \div 17 =$

Q12 $48 \div 6 =$

Q13 $35 \div 7 =$

Q14 $52 \div 13 =$

Q15 $112 \div 8 =$

Q16 $78 \div 13 =$

Q17 $90 \div 18$

Q18 $54 \div 9 =$

Q19 $135 \div 9 =$

Q20 $76 \div 19$

Q21   21 per cent of 100 =

Q22   30 per cent of 50 =

Q23   25 per cent of 10 =

Q24   20 per cent of 75 =

Q25   7 per cent of 300 =

Q26   12.5 per cent of 200 =

Q27   10 per cent of 120 =

Q28   1 per cent of 250 =

Q29   60 per cent of 400 =

Q30   3 per cent of 2,400 =

Q31   1 per cent of 1 =

Q32   6,000 × 8 per cent =

Q33   50 per cent of 2 =

Q34   0.5 × 50 per cent =

Q35   5,000 × 7 per cent =

Q36   10 per cent of 1 =

Q37   3 per cent of 20 =

Q38   5 per cent of 10 =

Q39   1 × 0.5 per cent =

Q40   15 × 6 per cent =

Q41   10,000 × 1 per cent =

Q42   40 per cent of 1 =

Q43   7,000 × 6 per cent =

Q44   80 × 15 per cent =

Q45   15 × 90 per cent =

Q46   4 per cent of 1 =

Q47   8,800 × 100 per cent =

Q48   25 × 20 per cent =

Q49   160 × 30 per cent =

Q50   120 × 25 per cent =

Using numbers and time

In the real test you face a test using numbers and time. It may well comprise a situation different from the one described here, but the skills required here are likely to be very similar to those needed in some real tests. Make sure that you can do this type of question really quickly, getting them right every time without a calculator.

Situation 1
The following situation relates to the 15 questions below it:

Imagine that a firefighter is allocated a response time that starts when an emergency call is received (time of call). The response time varies depending on the location of the incident and the time of day (think of this as the time allowed). Your task is to calculate the amount of time the firefighter has left in order to complete the task in the response time.

Consider the following example and then practise on the questions that follow:

Q1   Time of call: 11.00

Response time: 46 minutes
Time now: 11.20
Time left?

Answer ☐

Answer: 26 minutes

Explanation: the firefighter has 46 minutes in which to respond to the incident beginning from the time of the call. The call was received at 11.00 and the time now is 11.20, so 20 minutes of the response time has passed. This means that the firefighter has 26 minutes left.

Now try these examples:

Q2 Time of call: 08.11

Response time: 67 minutes
Time now: 08.52
Time left?

Answer [ ]

Q3 Time of call: 06.53

Response time: 41 minutes
Time now: 07.28
Time left?

Answer [ ]

Q4 Time of call: 03.37

Response time: 39 minutes
Time now: 04.06
Time left?

Answer [ ]

Q5 Time of call: 04.49

Response time: 44 minutes
Time now: 05.21
Time left?

Answer [ ]

Q6 Time of call: 01.39

Response time: 49 minutes
Time now: 02.18
Time left?

Answer [ ]

Q7   Time of call: 03.03

Response time: 99 minutes
Time now: 03.47
Time left?

Answer [   ]

Q8   Time of call: 11.51

Response time: 48 minutes
Time now: 12.15
Time left?

Answer [   ]

Q9   Time of call: 09.41

Response time: 40 minutes
Time now: 10.13
Time left?

Answer [   ]

Q10   Time of call: 07.04

Response time: 98 minutes
Time now: 08.41
Time left?

Answer [   ]

Q11   Time of call: 04.35

Response time: 57 minutes
Time now: 05.19
Time left?

Answer [   ]

Q12   Time of call: 03.50

Response time: 59 minutes
Time now: 04.29
Time left?

Answer [   ]

Q13   Time of call: 05.52

Response time: 71 minutes
Time now: 06.44
Time left?

Answer [   ]

Q14   Time of call: 07.21

Response time: 71 minutes
Time now: 08.17
Time left?

Answer [   ]

Q15   Time of call: 08.37

Response time: 54 minutes
Time now: 09.12
Time left?

Answer [   ]

More using numbers and time

Situation 2

Imagine a firefighter crew leaving the station to attend an incident. Your task in this situation is to calculate how long the crew have been at the incident. You are given the time that they departed the station (departure time), the time now and the time it took to reach the incident (journey time).

Consider the following example and then try the 14 examples that follow.

Remember a calculator is not allowed. Give all answers in minutes.

Q1   Departure time: 09.00

Time now: 10.10
Journey time: 15 minutes
Time in attendance?

Answer   [   ]

Answer: 55 minutes

Explanation: the crew left the station at 09.00 and took 15 minutes to reach the incident. They arrived at the incident therefore at 09.15. The time now is 10.10 so they have so far been at the incident for 55 minutes.

Q2   Departure time: 11.00

Time now: 12.20
Journey time: 30 minutes
Time in attendance?

Answer   [   ]

Q3   Departure time: 03.20

Time now: 05.09
Journey time: 16 minutes
Time in attendance?

Answer   [   ]

Q4   Departure time: 07.50

Time now: 08.17
Journey time: 9 minutes
Time in attendance?

Answer   [   ]

Q5   Departure time: 01.40

Time now: 02.33
Journey time: 21 minutes
Time in attendance?

Answer   [   ]

Q6 Departure time: 07.31

Time now: 09.11
Journey time: 36 minutes
Time in attendance?

Answer [   ]

Q7 Departure time: 09.10

Time now: 11.03
Journey time: 45 minutes
Time in attendance?

Answer [   ]

Q8 Departure time: 01.56

Time now: 02.40
Journey time: 29 minutes
Time in attendance?

Answer [   ]

Q9 Departure time: 10.07

Time now: 11.06
Journey time: 31 minutes
Time in attendance?

Answer [   ]

Q10 Departure time: 07.18

Time now: 08.31
Journey time: 7 minutes
Time in attendance?

Answer [   ]

Q11 Departure time: 11.01

Time now: 12.34
Journey time: 49 minutes
Time in attendance?

Answer [   ]

Q12   Departure time: 12.53
Time now: 01.40
Journey time: 22 minutes
Time in attendance?

Answer

Q13   Departure time: 08.13
Time now: 09.44
Journey time: 17 minutes
Time in attendance?

Answer

Q14   Departure time: 09.54
Time now: 10.18
Journey time: 23 minutes
Time in attendance?

Answer

Q15   Departure time: 11.07
Time now: 12.45
Journey time: 31 minutes
Time in attendance?

Answer

Even more using numbers and time

Situation 3

Imagine that you are allocated tasks and a time in which to complete them. This exercise requires that you work out from the information given how much time remains in which to complete the task. You are given the following information: time allowed, the time you started and the time now. Try the following 15 examples.

Give all answers in minutes. Remember you are working out the time that remains.

Q1   Time allowed: 60 minutes

Time at start: 08.15
Time now: 08.31
Time remaining?

Answer [   ]

Q2   Time allowed: 70 minutes

Time at start: 08.17
Time now: 09.21
Time remaining?

Answer [   ]

Q3   Time allowed: 50 minutes

Time at start: 03.40
Time now: 04.15
Time remaining?

Answer [   ]

Q4   Time allowed: 100 minutes

Time at start: 01.16
Time now: 02.31
Time remaining?

Answer [   ]

Q5   Time allowed: 80 minutes

Time at start: 08.27
Time now: 09.13
Time remaining?

Answer [   ]

Q6   Time allowed: 1 hour

Time at start: 11.41
Time now: 12.19
Time remaining?

Answer [   ]

Q7   Time allowed: 53 minutes

Time at start: 03.37
Time now: 04.24
Time remaining?

Answer [ ]

Q8   Time allowed: 120 minutes

Time at start: 05.21
Time now: 07.08
Time remaining?

Answer [ ]

Q9   Time allowed: 150 minutes

Time at start: 09.18
Time now: 10.43
Time remaining?

Answer [ ]

Q10   Time allowed: 46 minutes

Time at start: 08.51
Time now: 09.17
Time remaining?

Answer [ ]

Q11   Time allowed: 62 minutes

Time at start: 03.35
Time now: 04.21
Time remaining?

Answer [ ]

Q12   Time allowed: 28 minutes

Time at start: 11.45
Time now: 12.13
Time remaining?

Answer [ ]

Q13 Time allowed: 1 hour

Time at start: 04.51
Time now: 05.21
Time remaining?

Answer [   ]

Q14 Time allowed: 180 minutes

Time at start: 09.20
Time now: 10.53
Time remaining?

Answer [   ]

Q15 Time allowed: 2 hours

Time at start: 12.06
Time now: 01.57
Time remaining?

Answer [   ]

Using numbers: other operations you must master

Much of this chapter has been taken up with ensuring that you are confident and accurate in key operations and calculations that involve time. To succeed in the firefighter written test you must also be confident and accurate in the calculation of areas and distance, the interpretation of graphs and other visually presented numerical data, and in using numerical information to solve problems. Below you will find 40 practice questions to help you revise these other important skills. Complete them without the help of a calculator. If you need further practice of this sort then you will find hundreds more examples in the Kogan Page title *The Numeracy Test Workbook*.

Q1   Paul runs 50 lengths of the pitch each day and the pitch is 75 m long. How far does he run each day?

A.   More than 3.5 km

B.   More than 4 km

C.   Less than 3 km

D.   Between 3 and 3.5 km

Answer [   ]

Q2   What is the area of a room 6 m wide by 7 m long?

A. $30 \, m^2$

B. $36 \, m^2$

C. $42 \, m^2$

D. $49 \, m^2$

Answer [   ]

Q3   You need to pump out a flooded basement. How many 10 m lengths of hose will you need if it must reach 60 m along the street to a suitable storm drain, 20 m through to the back of the building and down a 10 m long stairwell to the water?

A.   9 lengths
B.   10 lengths
C.   90 m
D.   100 m

Answer [   ]

Q4   Sam swims 30 lengths of a 40 m pool each day. How far does she swim in seven days?

A.   8 km
B.   8.2 km
C.   8.4 km
D.   8.6 km

Answer [   ]

Q5   Which of the suggested dimensions could be a room with an area of 36 m²?

A.   9 m × 4 m
B.   7 m × 5 m
C.   8 m × 6 m
D.   6 m × 7 m

Answer [   ]

Q6   Each floor of the stairway to a tower block is 18 m long and hose is available in 15 m lengths. If you have 20 lengths of hose, how many floors up the tower block can you run the hose?

A.   15
B.   16
C.   17
D.   18

Answer [   ]

Q7   Jo spends 20 minutes rowing at an average of 18 km an hour. What distance does she cover?

A.   5 km
B.   6 km
C.   7 km
D.   8 km

Answer [   ]

Q8   Rain or shine Jon cycles every day and covers 28 km a week. How far does he cycle on an average day?

A.   3 km
B.   4 km
C.   5 km
D.   6 km

Answer [   ]

Q9   What is the combined area occupied by three rooms if their dimensions are 6 m × 6 m, 7 m × 7 m and 4 m × 3 m?

A.   94 m^2
B.   95 m^2
C.   96 m^2
D.   97 m^2

Answer [   ]

Q10   The nearest hydrant is 90 m along the street, and the fire is in a shed at the bottom of a 30 m garden. You will have to bring the hose through the house, which is 16 m in depth. Hose is available in 20 m lengths. How many lengths of hose will you need to reach the fire?

A.   5
B.   6
C.   7
D.   8

Answer [   ]

Situation 1

Year	All emergencies (all calls including false alarms)	False alarms	Injuries
2007	2,000	350	300
2006	1,840	310	275
2005	2,260	238	319

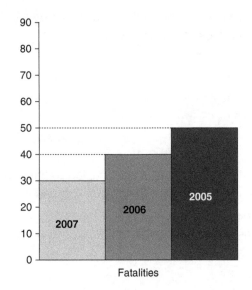

Fatalities

Use this information to answer the following three questions.

Q11 How many more fatalities occurred in 2007 and 2006 combined than in 2005?

A. 20
B. 21
C. 22
D. 23

Answer ☐

Q12 Over the three-year period, what was the total number of fatalities and injuries?

A. 894
B. 1,014
C. 1,044
D. 1,114

Answer [   ]

Q13 How many genuine emergency calls (not false alarms) were received over the three-year period?

A. 6,100
B. 6,002
C. 5,400
D. 5,202

Answer [   ]

Q14 If an auditorium comprises only seating for the audience and a 64 m² stage, what area does the seating occupy if the dimensions of the auditorium are: 14 m × 12 m?

A. 108 m²
B. 104 m²
C. 64 m²
D. 168 m²

Answer [   ]

Q15 To raise money for charity Jack must swim 5 km. So far he has covered 3 km in the 120 lengths he has swum. How many more lengths must he do?

A. 200
B. 120
C. 80
D. 40

Answer [   ]

Q16   A lake occupies an area of 470 m^2. Adjacent to it is a square area of land, one side of which is 14 m long. What is the combined area occupied by both the lake and the piece of land?

A.   555 m^2
B.   666 m^2
C.   777 m^2
D.   It is not possible to say

Answer

Situation 2

A survey of age

Your
neighbourhood

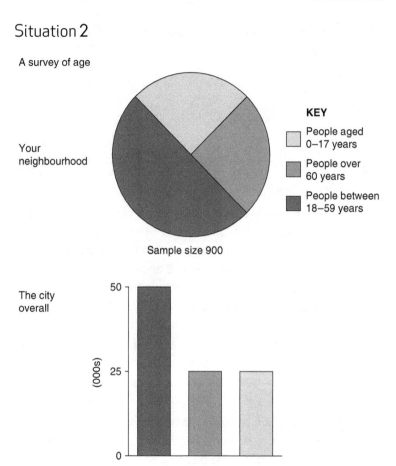

KEY

People aged
0–17 years

People over
60 years

People between
18–59 years

Sample size 900

The city
overall

(000s)

Use this information to answer the following three questions.

Q17 Which range, if any, gives the best estimate of the number of
people in the survey from your neighbourhood who are aged
over 60 years?

    A. 0–150

    B. 151–300

    C. 301–450

    D. It is not possible to say

Answer

Q18   How many people in the city overall are aged 0–59 years?

   A.   750
   B.   50,000
   C.   75,000
   D.   It is not possible to say

   Answer [   ]

Q19   From the information given, which of the following statements is true?

   A.   You can only estimate that half the people in 'your neighbourhood' are aged between 18 and 59 years.
   B.   You can only estimate that half the people in the city overall are aged between 18 and 59 years.
   C.   You can estimate that half the people in both your neighbourhood and the city overall are aged 18–59 years.
   D.   You can estimate that it is not true that half the people in both your neighbourhood and the city overall are aged 18–59 years.

   Answer [   ]

Q20   Each floor of a stairway is 8 m long and hose is available in 30 m lengths. How many lengths of hose will you require to reach the 9th floor of the block?

   A.   2   B.   3
   C.   4   D.   5

   Answer [   ]

Q21   Trish likes to swim 4 km a week and this means completing 50 lengths at her local swimming pool. How long is the pool at which she swims?

   A.   20 m   B.   40 m
   C.   60 m   D.   80 m

   Answer [   ]

Situation 3

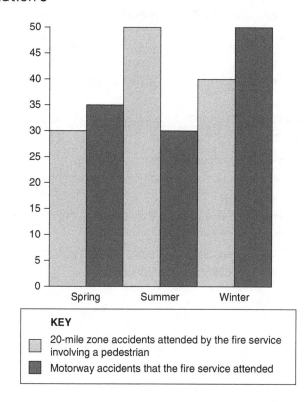

KEY

20-mile zone accidents attended by the fire service involving a pedestrian

Motorway accidents that the fire service attended

Use this information to answer the following three questions.

Q22 How many motorway accidents did the Fire Service attend over the period covered?

A. 115
B. 120
C. 125
D. 130

Answer

Q23 How many more summer than winter incidents involving pedestrians in 20-mile zones did the Fire Service attend?

A. 50   B. 40
C. 20   D. 10

Answer [   ]

Q24 Use the information given to identify which one of the following statements is true.

A. Motorways appear safest in the spring.
B. The majority of accidents involving pedestrians occur in the summer.
C. The Fire Service attends more accidents on motorways than in 20-mile zones.
D. The figures show that the Fire Service attended the fewest accidents in the spring.

Answer [   ]

Q25 You have 10 lengths of hose and each is 15 m long. Which floor of a nine-storey tower block could you reach if each floor requires 20 m of hose?

A. 9th   B. 8th
C. 7th   D. 6th

Answer [   ]

Q26 Jane averages 16 km an hour when running on her exercise machine. She usually runs for 15 minutes at a time. How many sessions on her running machine would she have to undertake to cover 40 km?

A. 8   B. 9
C. 10   D. 11

Answer [   ]

Situation 4

Household fires in England and Wales

Time of fire \ Location of fire	Kitchen	Bedroom	Living room	Other location
At night	200	105	80	140
During the day	350	80	160	60

Household fires in Scotland

Time of fire \ Location of fire	Kitchen	Bedroom	Living room	Other location
At night	90	75	87	70
During the day	150	40	50	30

Use the information to answer the following three questions.

Q27 How many household kitchen fires occur in England and Wales?

A. 200
B. 350
C. 550
D. 790

Answer [   ]

Q28 How many household fires occur in Scotland?

A. 322
B. 592
C. 1,175
D. 1,772

Answer [   ]

Q29 If a third of all kitchen fires in Scotland were caused by washing machines, how many in that region had a cause other than a washing machine?

A. 60   B. 80

C. 120   D. 160

Answer [ ]

Q30 You have five lengths of hose and each is 30 m long. Which storey of a nine-storey tower block could you reach if each floor requires 20 m of hose?

A. 5th   B. 6th

C. 7th   D. 8th

Answer [ ]

Q31 You visit the site of a recent fire. It is a large site taken up mostly by a warehouse and there is a terrible mess. Half the roof has collapsed, leaving an area 40 m by 150 m fully exposed to the elements. Calculate the total area occupied by the warehouse.

A. 6,000 m²

B. 8,000 m²

C. 10,000 m²

D. 12,000 m²

Answer [ ]

Q32 You and five colleagues go for a 5-km run every Sunday morning. How many Sundays will it take to cover a total of 300 km?

A. 9   B. 10

C. 11   D. 12

Answer [ ]

Situation 5

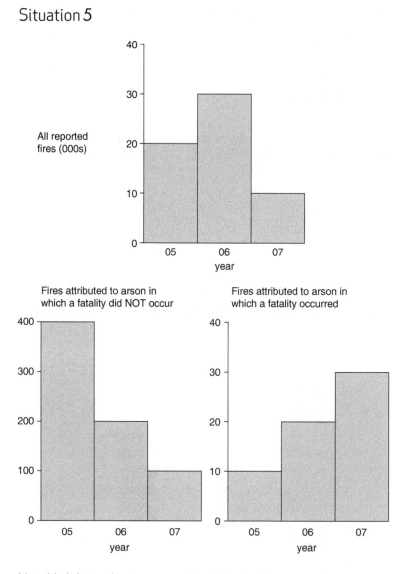

Use this information to answer the following three questions.

Q33 How many fires were reported over the three-year period?

A. 60

B. 6,000

C. 60,000

D. 66,000

Answer [   ]

Q34 How many fires over the three-year period were attributed to arson?

A. 700

B. 760

C. 820

D. 880

Answer [   ]

Q35 How many reported fires occurred that were NOT attributed to arson?

A. 59,240

B. 59,230

C. 59,220

D. 59,210

Answer [   ]

Q36 You have six lengths of hose and each is 20 m long. Which floor of a 12-storey tower block could you reach if each floor requires 15 m of hose?

A. 6

B. 7

C. 8

D. 9

Answer [   ]

Q37 Your ambition is to run a 26-mile marathon and you have been training for weeks; in the remaining time you aim to complete a run equivalent to a third of the full distance and then two half-marathons. How many miles will you cover in these final three runs and the full marathon?

A. Less than 57 miles
B. Less than 58 miles
C. Almost 60 miles
D. Over 60 miles

Answer [   ]

Situation 6

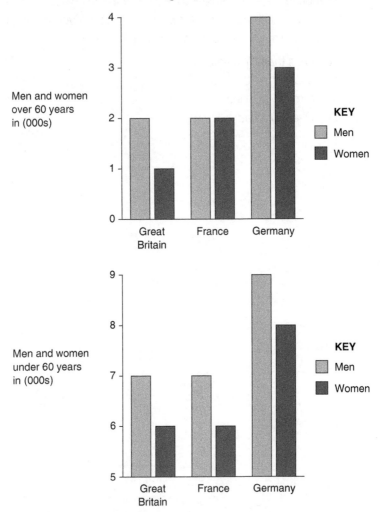

Men and women living alone who suffer a fire at home

Use this information to answer the following three questions.

Q38 How many men under 60 years of age living alone in Germany suffer a fire at home?

A. 800

B. 900

C. 1,700

D. 4,000

Answer

Q39 In total how many people live alone in the UK and suffer a fire in their home?

A. 4,300

B. 3,400

C. 3,000

D. 1,300

Answer

Q40 How many more people in Germany than France live alone, are over the age of 60 years and suffer a fire in their home?

A. 5,000

B. 4,000

C. 3,000

D. 2,000

Answer

The situational awareness paper

Most authorities are using the new written test structure that includes a paper titled 'Situational awareness and problem solving'. Situational awareness tests comprise a passage in which an imaginary workplace situation is described and list suggested responses to that situation. A lot of applicant firefighters find this part of the assessment a real challenge. Your task is to read the scenario (situation) and identify the suggested response that is most appropriate in the circumstances described.

You will find below 66 practice questions for this paper. They are organized as four sorts of practice. In the first 26 questions your task is to identify either the most appropriate, acceptable or less than acceptable suggested responses. However, there are more suggested responses than categories in which you can rank them. This means that you must rank more than one response the same. Enter your rankings in the answer matrix. The next 13 questions are intended to get you thinking about priorities and getting them in the order that the Fire Service expects. This is followed by seven questions formatted in a way similar to the real thing so you can get used to answering this style of question. The last 20 questions are organized as a realistic practice test.

The first 26 situational awareness questions

It is important that you realize that the 26 situational awareness questions below are in a different style from the questions you will encounter in the real test. This is intentional because, while these questions require a different way of working, they will help you think about the priorities and approach that the Fire Service is looking for and so help you prepare for the challenge of the real firefighter situational awareness paper. Master this style of question, then move on to the remaining 40 questions in this chapter and you will be ready for the challenge of the real applicant firefighter situational awareness test.

Remember your task is to rank the suggested responses as either the most appropriate, acceptable or less than acceptable, and you must rank more than one response the same. Be sure that you only refer to the information provided in the situation. In other words, use only your own best judgement and the information provided to decide the rankings.

Identify as the most appropriate the response that you consider is the best of those suggested. If you consider two or more of the suggested responses the most appropriate, then do not rank any of the answers as A but instead rank them both as B, an acceptable response. It is possible that you do not consider any of the suggested responses the most appropriate or acceptable; in that case do not rank any of the answers as A or B and instead rank them all as C. The answer and explanation to the first situation and question is provided below as an example.

Answers and explanations are provided in Chapter 6. To score your answers to these 26 questions award yourself a maximum of 4 marks per question, one mark for each correct ranking that you attribute to each suggested response. Note that it is very unlikely that you will rank all the responses as suggested in the answers. So don't be too hard on yourself and consider yourself as doing very well if you can score over 65 out of the maximum score of 104.

Situation 1

Simon – one of your watch colleagues – told you that watch leader Micky was receiving text messages and written notes from a secret admirer. Paul on your watch told you that it was Lynn on blue watch who was sending them as he heard her discussing it. He had heard her say that no matter what she suggested Micky was saying no. That did not surprise you as you knew that Micky has been happily married for 26 years. Simon told Paul that Lynn should know better because she too was married and with a young family.

Q1   Rate the suggested responses as:

A. The most appropriate response
B. An acceptable response
C. A less than acceptable response

The suggested responses

1 Talk to your boss and ask her if she has a suggestion on how to deal with distracting work rumours.

2 Let the rumour run its course and die on its own.

3 Tell those that gossip that you don't want any part of the rumour.

4 Ask them to stop spreading rumours and gossip.

Your answer

1	2	3	4
B	C	B	B

Explanation: rumours have no place at work. They distract everyone from performing their expected duties, resulting in a less productive work day, cause unnecessary conflict and are detrimental to employee relations and morale. Suggested responses 1, 3 and 4 would help stop the rumour, so are acceptable responses. Suggested response 2 would not help stop it, so is a less than acceptable response.

Situation 2

You are the only black person in the company and you believe you are being treated differently from your colleagues because you are only offered the unpopular shifts and denied the overtime everyone else is offered. Your fears are confirmed when colleagues start calling you names that are obviously a reference to your ethnic origin. Your confidence is low, you feel humiliated and physically sick.

Q2 Rate the suggested responses as:

A. The most appropriate response
B. An acceptable response
C. A less than acceptable response

The suggested responses

1 Say and do nothing, because if you do not react the name calling will fail in its purpose and people will get bored with it.

2 Talk to colleagues who might be suffering the same problems and, if they are, work out what you can do about it together.

3 Keep a diary of events of who said what, when, circumstances and any witnesses. This will give a vital record of the nature of the racism you are facing.

4 Find out whether your employer has specific rules about racism at work or a grievance procedure you can use to raise the issue and try to solve the problem.

Your answer

1	2	3	4

Situation 3

> The work is dirty, the washing facilities are rudimentary and there is nowhere to store your clothes so that you can wear the protective clothing provided. Nor is there an area for rest breaks and eating meals, so you stand around during breaks and eat where you can. When it rains you all get wet. None of your co-workers are women and the general public are not allowed on site, so you don't believe there is any need to provide somewhere private to get changed or suitable facilities for pregnant women or nursing mothers. However, you do believe that your employers should provide better facilities or at least some sort of facilities. You have discussed this with them more than once but you are just dismissed as a troublemaker.

Q3 Rate the suggested responses as:

  A. The most appropriate response
  B. An acceptable response
  C. A less than acceptable response

The suggested responses

1 Try talking informally again with your employer about the inadequate working conditions.

2 Do nothing, because only businesses employing five or more people must have facilities for staff to change, rest and eat.

3 Refuse to work until facilities are improved and not worry about being threatened with disciplinary action because an industrial tribunal would be bound to agree that conditions were inadequate.

4 Raise the matter in writing with your employer, outlining your concerns and how you believe things might be arranged differently.

	1	2	3	4
Your answer				

Situation 4

I have a few strong beliefs, especially when it comes to the welfare of animals, but this does not normally affect my working relationship with colleagues. Last week however during a tea break I found myself in a heated argument when a colleague said it was OK to drown unwanted kittens in a bucket. Things got a bit out of hand and I guess we all said things we didn't really mean. Except for essential work-related communication we have not spoken since. I feel upset and stressed by the situation and it is affecting my work.

Q4   Rate the suggested responses as:

   A.   The most appropriate response
   B.   An acceptable response
   C.   A less than acceptable response

The suggested responses

1 I would try to resolve things informally with my co-workers, and if that did not work then I would next raise the matter informally with my supervisor to see if she could help resolve matters.

2 The first thing I would do is write a letter to my employer setting out the details of the grievance I have with my co-workers.

3 I would ask my employer if I could be transferred to another section, and if this was not possible I would tender my resignation.

4 I would try talking with my employer informally to see if there was anything they could do to improve the situation. If that did not work I would raise a formal grievance against my colleagues.

Your answer	1	2	3	4

Situation 5

> You were attending to a flooded building. It was the known haunt of drug dealers and only a few weeks ago you had attended it to put out a deliberately started fire. Your crew set up the pumps to clear the water and as usual with a flooding there was a terrible mess; once the water was clear the crew set about a final careful search to be sure that there were no casualties and to make sure that what property could be salvaged is saved. You were all helping with the search when you noticed one of your colleagues put something in his pocket. You can't be 100 per cent certain but it looked like a wad of money. You said nothing at that stage because you assumed he would hand it to the watch leader once the search was complete but to your amazement he did not. Later you approached him and told him what you saw. He replied that it was bound to be the property of a drug dealer and such a person is not exactly going to come forward and claim the money as theirs, so he saw no point in handing it in.

Q5 Rate the suggested responses as:

A. The most appropriate response
B. An acceptable response
C. A less than acceptable response

The suggested responses

1 Ask how much he had found and ask if you can have some of it.

2 Congratulate him on his good luck.

3 Go directly to your watch leader and tell him what you saw and what your colleague said.

4 Explain that you consider his action entirely inappropriate and that if he does not hand the money to your watch leader by the end of the shift you will tell your watch leader what you saw and what was said.

Your answer	1	2	3	4

Situation 6

Your wife is Nigerian and she is looking for work. She showed you a job advert that she found in the Local Job Centre to work as a machine operative on an assembly line and she wanted to apply, but the advert said that all applicants must have a high standard of spoken English. Your wife's English is good and she understands everything but you would not describe her as having a high standard of spoken English as she speaks with a quite strong accent and makes grammatical mistakes from time to time.

Q6   Rate the suggested responses as:

A.   The most appropriate response
B.   An acceptable response
C.   A less than acceptable response

The suggested responses

1 Contact the employer and explain that you believe the advertisement to be unfair as working on a production line does not require a high standard of spoken English.

2 Suggest that your wife submits an application anyway, including an explanation that she believes her command of English is sufficient to do the job properly.

3 Take a copy of the advert and attach it to a letter of complaint addressed to the manager of the job centre, explaining that you believe the advert to be indirectly discriminatory because work on a production line does not require a high standard of spoken English.

4 Explain to your wife that employers have every right to specify that applicants must have a high standard of spoken English.

Your answer	1	2	3	4

Situation 7

> The only complaint I had about my job was that there was too much of it.
> I simply couldn't get everything done without stretching and stressing myself.
> Things got even worse with the recession. The company undertook a major
> cost-saving exercise and this meant even more for me to do and less
> support. I found it harder and harder to keep up with my workload and in
> the end I went to my doctor and he diagnosed a stress-related illness.
> He signed me off work for a month.

Q7   Rate the suggested responses as:

   A.   The most appropriate response
   B.   An acceptable response
   C.   A less than acceptable response

The suggested responses

1 Before I returned to work I would write to my manager
   informing him that my illness was stress related and that
   I believed that it was caused by my workload, and ask
   for my job to be changed so that the workload was more
   reasonable.

2 When I returned to work I would take care that I always
   took lunch breaks and left on time.

3 At the end of my period of sick leave I would go back to
   my doctor and seek a further period off work.

4 Before returning to work I would write to my manager to
   inform him that I believed my stress-related illness was
   caused by the amount of work I was expected to
   undertake and ask to meet with him so that we might
   discuss ways in which my job might be reorganized to
   avoid the risk of my falling ill again.

Your answer	1	2	3	4

Situation 8

A bereavement is something we all face at some stage or another. Even when it is expected after a long period of ill health, it is still a terrible thing to have to deal with. When the person who dies is close to you, then it affects everything. When it is your husband or wife, then your private life is obviously turned upside down and how your friends and relatives relate to you is somehow different following the death. Going back to work after such a bereavement often helps: it keeps you busy and helps make things seem more normal. At least that is what you thought, but in your experience work soon became too much and you found it harder and harder to cope. In the end you felt you really needed to speak to your boss about how you felt, and during the conversation you found that you could not hide your feelings any longer and you broke down in tears.

Q8   Rate the suggested responses as:

A. The most appropriate response
B. An acceptable response
C. A less than acceptable response

The suggested responses

1 You would compose yourself as much as possible and continue with the conversation.

2 You would apologize and close the meeting.

3 You would compose yourself, ask your boss to make no allowances for your situation and as much as possible to ensure everything at work is as it was before the bereavement.

4 You would take as much time as is required to compose yourself and then explore practical ways in which your workload might be adjusted to take into account your situation.

Your answer	1	2	3	4

Situation 9

Made a mistake

Your manager asked you to take a vital spare part for a hydraulic pump to a fire station in Manchester. The spare that your fire authority had was the nearest available and so you collected the part and got on the train to make the 30-mile journey. The train arrived at Manchester ahead of time and it took you a bit by surprise to see the name of the station, so you disembarked in a hurry, only to realize moments too late that you had left the spare part behind on the seat next to you. You chased the train down the platform shouting for it to stop, but of course it did not. You ran to the station manager's office and explained what you had done. They phoned ahead and arranged for someone to board the train at the next stop to recover the item. If it could be found they explained that it would be held and you could take the next train up the line to collect it. You had never felt so foolish in all you life.

Q9   Rate the suggested responses as:

A. The most appropriate response

B. An acceptable response

C. A less than acceptable response

The suggested responses

1 You would catch the next train up the line, recover the item and return to deliver the part to the fire station in Manchester as you were instructed.

2 You would catch the next train, recover the item and then phone your manager to explain the situation.

3 You would ask the station manager to arrange for the item once recovered to be placed on the next train down the line and wait for it on the platform.

4 You would immediately phone your manager and tell him of your error and what actions you are taking to correct it.

Your answer	1	2	3	4

Situation 10

> My manager often smells of alcohol and it appears she is drinking during the day, which makes me very uncomfortable. She often does not seem to know what is going on and makes bizarre requests and decisions. She takes a lot of time off work and this puts extra pressure on us all as we end up with a different temporary manager each time. I feel senior management have left us in a chaotic situation and it is unfair to us to have to work in this atmosphere. I am finding it a major source of upset.

Q10 Rate the suggested responses as:

   A. The most appropriate response
   B. An acceptable response
   C. A less than acceptable response

The suggested responses

1 I would go to HR and ask to speak to them anonymously about the situation.

2 She obviously has a major problem so I would just try to put up with it.

3 I would approach one of the HR representatives and share my concerns in as professional and empathetic manner as I could.

4 I would approach her directly and discuss with her my suspicions and the upset her actions are causing.

Your answer

1	2	3	4

Situation 11

A colleague on your watch (you are both firefighters) tells you that when he is at work he takes care not to say the word, but the fact of the matter is he is a fireman and has been for a long time (he is due to retire in three years). He explains that the word that he cannot say is fireman because the fire authority will label him sexist if he says it. So when at the station he goes along with what he calls 'political correctness' and says firefighter but outside work he says fireman and he does not care who hears him.

Q11 Rate the suggested responses as:

    A. The most appropriate response

    B. An acceptable response

    C. A less than acceptable response

The suggested responses

1 You would explain that the problem with the term fireman is that it might discourage women from applying to be a firefighter and that for this reason we should avoid it, especially at work but also outside work.

2 Given that your colleague will only use the term fireman outside work, you see nothing wrong with what he has to say.

3 Your colleague is due to retire in three years and you know that the service is very different today from how it was when he first joined, so you would make an exception and not make an issue of what he says.

4 You would tell him that he should care who hears him because even when outside work a firefighter should uphold the principle that both men and women can be firefighters and language that suggests otherwise should be avoided.

Your answer	1	2	3	4

Situation 12

I was one of the crew that attended an incident where two children tragically died. The story was extensively covered by local TV and radio. The two sisters were caught in a burning car in which they were travelling and the heat was just too intense for their father to reach them. He tried repeatedly and was badly burned but each time he was beaten back. By the time we got there it was too late for us to do anything but recover their burned bodies. No matter how many times I see that sort of thing it always affects me and I find the death of children the hardest to deal with. Talking about it helps, and after work a few of us went out together and one of our group got into a conversation with someone he knew and they got talking about the tragedy.

Q12 Rate the suggested responses as:

A. The most appropriate response

B. An acceptable response

C. A less than acceptable response

The suggested responses

1 Given that it was already on the news and in the papers, I wouldn't do anything.

2 I would join in the conversation and offer my perspective on the tragedy.

3 I would interrupt and stop the conversation.

4 Talking helps, so I would encourage all of the team to discuss the events with anyone they wished.

Your answer

1	2	3	4

Situation 13

A community representative who does not speak English

> Our fire station holds a series of community open days when representatives from all sorts of local organizations and groups can have a look around and can see what we do. At the last event a community elder from one of the minority communities attended but it was really difficult to explain things to her because she hardly spoke a word of English.

Q13 Rate the suggested responses as:

    A. The most appropriate response

    B. An acceptable response

    C. A less than acceptable response

The suggested responses

1 Raise with the station commander the possibility of organizing things differently next time so that members of the community who could not speak English could get more out of the day.

2 Contact the community group to which the elder belongs and suggest that next time they send someone along who can speak English.

3 Offer to contact the local authority's minority language unit in order to get the leaflets and handouts that are available at the open days translated into the community elder's language in time for the next open day.

4 Suggest to the station commander that before the next open day a contact at the fire station is provided so that anyone who wants to attend but who needs things organized differently (to deal with, for example, a disability or a language problem) can contact them and explain their special requirements in time for their needs to be accommodated.

Your answer	1	2	3	4

Situation 14

You noticed that two of your team who had previously worked well together had since a reorganization started to blame each other for even the slightest problem and now bicker over responsibilities.

Q14 Rate the suggested responses as:

A. The most appropriate response
B. An acceptable response
C. A less than acceptable response

The suggested responses

1 You would call a team meeting and re-communicate the roles assigned to each member of the team at the reorganization.

2 You would call a team meeting and explain that you have noticed that there seems to be some confusion over roles and responsibilities since the reorganization, and then re-communicate the roles assigned to each member of the team at the reorganization.

3 You would review the assignment of roles to see if there was any unintentional duplication or conflict, and meet with the two individuals to discuss what you have noticed and seek their views on whether or not the assignment of roles can be adjusted to avoid doubling-up or clash.

4 You would meet with the two individuals and re-communicate the roles assigned to them at the reorganization.

Your answer

1	2	3	4

Situation 15

> A visitor to your building reported that her mobile phone and packet of
> sweets went missing when she left a room that she was using to go to use
> the toilet facilities. There is a large sign in the room that states that personal
> belongings should not be left unattended and that management could not
> take any responsibility for any loss or damage to personal items. The room
> is covered by a security camera, and when you review the footage you
> observe a member of your staff entering the room and appear to pick up
> something from the table. You approach the member of staff, who confesses
> to taking the sweets but denies taking the mobile phone.

Q15   Rate the suggested responses as:

    A. The most appropriate response

    B. An acceptable response

    C. A less than acceptable response

The suggested responses

1 You would call the police and report the theft and tell
them that you have CCT footage that appears to identify
the thief and that a member of staff has admitted to
stealing one of the missing items.

2 You would insist that the individual replaces the sweets
and apologize to the visitor; you would also explain to the
visitor that there was nothing you could do about the phone
and remind them of the content of the sign in the room.

3 You would search the individual's desk and pockets to
see if you could locate the phone.

4 You would arrange for a meeting between the visitor and
the individual so that the staff member could explain that
he only took the sweets and apologize.

Your answer	1	2	3	4

Situation 16

> You criticize a member of your staff for grammatical errors in a report and he denies being the author. You realize that you were mistaken but he gets extremely angry and starts shouting and using bad language.

Q16 Rate the suggested responses as:

    A. The most appropriate response

    B. An acceptable response

    C. A less than acceptable response

The suggested responses

1 You would interrupt him to instruct him to stop shouting and using bad language, and you would tell him that when he has calmed down you wish to speak to him; you would then turn away and leave him.

2 You would let him have his say and then apologize and retract your criticism.

3 You would let him finish and calmly tell him not to shout and swear, and then you would apologize and retract your criticism.

4 You would interrupt to stop him and explain that you wished to apologize for your error but that it is entirely unacceptable for him to shout and use bad language. You say that if he does not stop immediately you will walk away and discuss the matter with him later.

Your answer

1	2	3	4

Situation 17

You overhear a heated conversation between two members of staff, neither of whom is in your team. You are shocked to hear one of them threaten the other with physical violence. You know both the individuals concerned and can't really believe what you are hearing. Soon after the threat the individuals become aware of your presence and the conversation abruptly stops.

Q17 Rate the suggested responses as:

    A. The most appropriate response
    B. An acceptable response
    C. A less than acceptable response

The suggested responses

1 You would act as if you had heard nothing and not get involved.

2 You would take the matter up according to the procedure laid down in the staff handbook.

3 You would approach their respective line managers and report the matter to them.

4 You would speak to the two individuals, tell them what you heard and explain that you consider it a very serious matter and something they need to sort out between themselves without resort to threats of violence.

Your answer

1	2	3	4

Situation 18

A colleague complains to you about the body odour of a member of your team. On a few occasions you have noticed the bad odour yourself but decided against saying anything as you are aware of some personal difficulties that the individual faces.

Q18 Rate the suggested responses as:

A. The most appropriate response

B. An acceptable response

C. A less than acceptable response

The suggested responses

1 You would quietly explain to your colleague the nature of the personal problems that the individual faces and ask them to be more understanding.

2 Resolve to raise the matter with the individual at the next team meeting and inform your colleague that you will handle it.

3 Ask your colleague to say no more on the subject and do nothing.

4 Meet privately with the member of your team and ask that person to pay more attention to personal hygiene.

Your answer

1	2	3	4

Situation 19

One of the foremen at your place of work has a terrible reputation when it comes to how he treats his staff. for example he calls them 'boy', which the black members of his team say they find particularly offensive. He swears at them using really objectionable terms of a sexual nature that insult their mothers and sisters. Management know about it but they do nothing to stop it. You are so relieved that you do not work for him.

Q19   Rate the suggested responses as:

  A.   The most appropriate response
  B.   An acceptable response
  C.   A less than acceptable response

The suggested responses

1 Support your colleagues by trying to work out with them what they can do about the harassment.

2 Tell friends what is going on.

3 Find out whether your employer has specific rules about harassment at work or a grievance procedure, and encourage your colleagues to use them to raise the problem.

4 Offer to support your colleagues in an approach to your employer, at first informally but if this does not work then through a formal grievance.

Your answer

1	2	3	4

Situation 20
Very challenging member of the community

Elena would lose her cool over pretty much anything. It was impossible to know what the next trigger would be but the outcome was predictable and she would fly into a rage at some unfortunate person, making bizarre threats and largely incoherent assertions. It was a mistake to try and reason with her, and if anyone did it was like pouring petrol on a bonfire; she would explode. Ordinarily this would not bother you but she was the chairperson of the local homeless persons' association and you had just been asked to liaise with the association to help ensure that their clients are made aware of fire-safety issues. It was only the second time that you met with Elena and she took affront at your suggestion that she might want to receive copies of the latest Home Office literature on fire safety. Even though you had known at some stage she would lose her temper with you, the ferociousness of the assault left you speechless and upset.

Q20   Rate the suggested responses as:

A.   The most appropriate response

B.   An acceptable response

C.   A less than acceptable response

The suggested responses

1 I was prepared for this to happen so I would say nothing and continue to do my job in as professional a manner as possible.

2 As soon as she had stopped I would ask her why she reacted in such an inappropriate way towards my offer to provide the latest available literature.

3 I would explain that I would end the meeting immediately if she did not apologize and undertake not to speak to me in such a tone again.

4 I would explain that her behaviour was inappropriate, that the meeting was now closed and that I would be reporting back to my manager requesting that we write to the board of the association to make a formal complaint about her conduct.

Your answer

1	2	3	4

Situation 21

It was the birthday of one of your crew and you agreed to meet at the pub at the end of the shift for a drink. There was the usual banter and jokes going on and it was all light hearted and fun. However, you then heard someone tease Jane over her sexuality.

Q21   Rate the suggested responses as:

A.   The most appropriate response
B.   An acceptable response
C.   A less than acceptable response

The suggested responses

1 I would call the person who was teasing Jane an idiot and tell Jane to take no notice of the nonsense.

2 I would let Jane deal with it but explain to her afterwards that I witnessed the remark and if she needed me as a witness to make a formal complain at work the next day she need only ask.

3 If it had been in work, then what was said would have contravened our code of conduct and I would have backed Jane in bringing a grievance against the person if that was what she had wished to do. However, it was outside work so the code does not apply.

4 Harmless banter outside work is something we have to accept, but if it upsets you then you should tell the person that it does and they should refrain from it in the future.

Your answer

1	2	3	4

Situation 22

My job is really boring because I do not have enough to do. There are three people in our section and two people could easily do all the work. We spend a lot of the time sitting around chatting or surfing the internet and getting really bored. As a result I have lost all of the enthusiasm I used to have for my job and I feel like raising the matter with management, but my colleagues say I should not because it might mean that someone gets made redundant.

Q22 Rate the suggested responses as:
   A. The most appropriate response
   B. An acceptable response
   C. A less than acceptable response

The suggested responses

1 I would take the advice of my colleagues and not raise the matter with management.

2 I would look for another job; that way I might get my enthusiasm for my work back and save someone from losing their job.

3 If I was so bored that I had lost all enthusiasm in my work, then I would raise the matter with my manager.

4 I would ask for a meeting with my manager and ask for a greater workload.

Your answer

1	2	3	4

Situation 23

You work for the regional airport. Your employer is quarrying just beside the airport and crushing the recovered rock to form hardcore that is then used to expand the airport apron (the apron is where the planes stand when not in use). The airport gets really busy a couple of times a year and the extension of the apron must be finished in time for the next busy period. Key to the whole operation is a giant rock crusher, which is being operated 24/7 to ensure that enough hardcore is produced in time. Your employer has asked if you would operate the crusher for a shift as the usual operator has asked to take a day off. You know the machine is potentially very dangerous.

Q23 Rate the suggested responses as:

A. The most appropriate response
B. An acceptable response
C. A less than acceptable response

The suggested responses

1 I would ask the current operator to show me how to use the machine, and once I felt I had got the hang of it I would work the shift.

2 I would operate the machine as asked because, while the request is obviously dangerous, only businesses employing five or more people must have plans in place to deal with any risks.

3 I would refuse to work the machine as it was not safe for me to do so, and I would not worry about being threatened with disciplinary action because an employer can't make you do something unsafe.

4 I would explain that I was not suitably trained or experienced to work the rock crusher, but if they could organize the necessary training I would be happy to operate it.

Your answer	1	2	3	4

Situation 24

Annoying member of your team

Paul, like lots of people, believes that global warming threatens the existence of the human race. He spends a lot of his spare time visiting climate change websites and shares the latest views with the rest of the team. Some of your colleagues agree with him. Others either are not interested or respond negatively, sometimes just to wind him up. However he rarely talks about anything else and you all have become really fed up with his determination to convert you to his point of view. There have been a few stand-up rows and you and your colleagues have tried to agree a ban of all talk of climate change, but Paul is as determined as he is dogmatic and he will not let the subject drop. As far as he is concerned whoever disagrees with him is a denier of the obvious facts.

Q24 Rate the suggested responses as:

A. The most appropriate response

B. An acceptable response

C. A less than acceptable response

The suggested responses

1 I would take the matter up with my watch leader and ask if he could intervene and try to put a stop to the cause of the bad feeling.

2 I would suggest that we again all agree no more talk about climate change.

3 I would ask to be transferred to another watch.

4 I would go to the personnel officer and ask if there was anything he or she could do to help.

Your answer

1	2	3	4

Situation 25

Your wife of 12 years has left you, and most of your mutual friends found this out when – even though you are still man and wife – she posted on Facebook that she is single and had moved out of the family home. She has stopped wearing her wedding ring and is fooling around with other men. As much as you try, your marriage problems are impacting on your work. Colleagues who had read the Facebook message naturally asked you what was happening; others have started to comment on the change in your approach at work and you know it is only a matter of time before your watch leader will ask you if everything is ok.

Q25 Rate the suggested responses as:

A. The most appropriate response
B. An acceptable response
C. A less than acceptable response

The suggested responses

1 I would try even harder to ensure that my family problems do not impact on my job.

2 I would tell my co-workers and watch leader nothing. That way my personal problems can't affect my work.

3 I would tell my watch leader about my problems and ask him not to share them with anyone else, and where practical to make allowances for the impact it was having on my work.

4 I would ask my co-workers and watch leader to please help me by keeping my private life separate from work.

Your answer

1	2	3	4

Situation 26

> Since you gave up volleyball, which you used to play competitively, you have struggled to keep your weight down and if you are honest to yourself you must be something like 8 or 9 kilos heavier than you were just two years ago. Now that you have a family you simply don't have the time anymore to work out at the gym or go for a run. Despite the extra weight you know that you are still perfectly able to do your job.

Q26 Rate the suggested responses as:

    A. The most appropriate response

    B. An acceptable response

    C. A less than acceptable response

The suggested responses

1 I am perfectly able to do my job so I would change nothing.

2 I would discuss it with my wife and kids, and seek their support to help me back into shape by finding time for me to exercise.

3 I would make an appointment to see the manager at the fire authority in charge of staff fitness and ask her to help me devise and stick to a programme of weight loss.

4 I would resolve to take up running again and to go to the gym again.

Your answer

1	2	3	4

End of test

Thirteen questions to get you thinking about priorities and getting them in the order that the Fire Service expects

Q1 Who would you help first?

A. People stuck in a lift between floors.

B. A distressed, elderly lady.

C. A drowning dog.

D. Someone trying to recover their lost property.

Answer [   ]

Q2 When would you not carry out an instruction?

A. When a situation was dangerous.

B. When something else arose that was very urgent.

C. When a situation became much more dangerous.

D. When you felt too tired to go on.

Answer [   ]

Q3 Which task would you leave till last?

A. Raise the alarm.

B. Evacuate the people.

C. Assess the spread and growth of the fire.

D. Fight the fire.

Answer [   ]

Q4 Who would you help first?

A. A man trapped by rising flood water.

B. A colleague who had broken his leg in a fall.

C. A screaming child separated from her parents.

D. A woman locked inside her car in a motorway car park.

Answer [   ]

Q5 When would you ask permission from someone in authority before you took action?

A. To assist a colleague who had become half-buried in burning wreckage.

B. Before you break down a locked door behind which you think someone may be trapped.

C. When you are evacuating a building and someone asks you to assist them to safety.

D. To remove combustible material that is about to go up in flames.

Answer _____

Q6 What task would you tackle second?

A. Assist anyone who could not leave the scene unassisted.

B. Identify an adequate means of escape.

C. Estimate the number of people trapped.

D. Start the evacuation of people.

Answer _____

Q7 When would you not deliberately risk your life?

A. To rescue a colleague.

B. To rescue a homeless person.

C. To save someone who is trying to commit suicide.

D. To rescue the body of a child.

Answer _____

Q8 When would you not necessarily tell someone in authority?

A. When a colleague failed to report back when expected.

B. When you rescue someone from a crashed vehicle faster than expected.

C. When you fear that a situation is deteriorating rapidly.

D. When you find some valuable property obviously abandoned by someone as they flee the scene.

Answer _____

Q9   Which fire would you tackle first?

    A.   A fire spreading fast through a deserted warehouse.

    B.   A fire in a school lit by arsonists in the early hours.

    C.   A fire producing an acrid smoke that is being blown across town.

    D.   A fire in a hospice (a hospice is a place where terminally ill people are cared for).

Answer [   ]

Q10   What would you do last?

    A.   Recover property.

    B.   Rescue an animal.

    C.   Help an elderly person to safety.

    D.   Put out a fire.

Answer [   ]

Q11   What would concern you most?

    A.   Telling a member of the public that their relative was still unaccounted for.

    B.   The fact that someone was very likely to be injured unless you quickly remove a fallen tree.

    C.   That the rapid spread of a fire was preventing you from recovering a person who had been overcome by smoke and died from the effects of the heat.

    D.   Confronting a menacing gang who were impeding your team's efforts to tackle an emergency.

Answer [   ]

Q12   What would you not worry about?

    A.   Taking risks.

    B.   An unavoidable delay in reaching an emergency.

    C.   Others taking risks.

    D.   Having to tell someone in authority that you had made a mistake.

Answer [   ]

Q13 When would you need help most urgently?

   A. In poor visibility you can hear a child crying but cannot find her.

   B. It is hours after the official end of your shift and your work at the incident is still far from completed.

   C. You are extracting someone from a crushed car while oncoming traffic is passing at speed close to the incident.

   D. The rapid spread of the fire is threatening to cut off your only means of escape.

   Answer _____

Seven questions in the format found in the real situations awareness paper

Q14 When on a workplace visit, you are asked to promote the business case for training all employees in how to prevent a fire from occurring in the first place and how to act should a fire occur. At a place of work you would remind the employer that:

   A. It makes good business sense to provide fire-safety training for their employees.

   B. Employers have a legal duty to provide fire-safety training to their staff.

   C. Fire kills.

   D. Fires at work are far more common than people realize.

   Answer _____

Q15   Your team is called to an incident on a motorway at night. You soon realize that there are casualties and that there are more vehicles involved than initially reported, because a number of vehicles have been shunted out of sight down an embankment into a fast-running stream. One of these vehicles is at risk of being submerged in the water. Should you first:

A.   Attend to the casualties and call for extra assistance.

B.   Get someone to radio for assistance, while the rest of the team investigate the submerged vehicle.

C.   Investigate the vehicle most at risk of being submerged.

D.   Split the team so that some attend to casualties while others investigate the submerged vehicle and someone calls for extra assistance.

Answer

Q16   It has been raining on and off all day and it looks like it could start raining again any minute. You have just started your lunch break and you are told to bring a delivery of goods into the storeroom when you have finished. Just as you start eating you see a van pull up and the driver unloading the goods outside the fire station. Would you:

A.   Continue eating and when you have finished go to collect the goods.

B.   Stop what you are doing and go to collect the goods.

C.   Wait until the end of your lunch break and then go to collect the goods.

D.   Tell the person that it is not in your job description to fetch and carry deliveries.

Answer

Q17 Your team is instructed to clean a fire appliance that has just returned to the station. It is very dirty and even if you work hard the job will take a long time to complete. As you work a member of the public approaches to speak to you. Would you:

A. Ask them to leave the premises before they get into trouble.

B. Continue working but listen to what they have to say.

C. Stop working to hear what they have to say.

D. Tell them that for their own safety they can't come in, and direct them to the office.

Answer ☐

Q18 Tom as usual is drunk and abusive. He has lived rough in the same place for as long as anyone can remember, and from the fire he has lit to keep warm, smoke is billowing across the road and presenting a hazard to the traffic. The trouble is that as soon as you leave the scene he will light another fire and in no time at all you will be called out again. Would you:

A. Have a whip round and give him the money to buy more alcohol so that he can drink more and fall asleep, which will keep him quiet for the rest of your watch.

B. Put out his fire and escort him away from the area and tell him not to go back.

C. Find him some material that will burn without creating smoke so he can keep warm and not endanger the traffic.

D. Put out his fire and remove any combustible material nearby and tell him that you will call the police if he lights another.

Answer ☐

Q19   Your team is the first to arrive at a fire in a museum of fine art. You find the fire is threatening the priceless collection of work, which will be destroyed if you do not act fast; however, there are reports that a night watchman is still in the large building. Should you:

A.   Search for the night watchman and let the art burn.

B.   Tackle the fire and save the priceless collection.

C.   Split your team into two and try to do both.

D.   Radio for advice on what to do.

Answer [   ]

Q20   You feel that you are not getting sufficient opportunity to keep physically fit because the gym equipment at the station is nearly always being used and your family commitments leave little or no opportunity to train in your own time. Would you:

A.   Accept the fact that it is not always possible to do everything.

B.   Complain to you team mates about the inadequate facilities at the station.

C.   Ask your line manager if there is anything that can be done to improve matters.

D.   Suggest a rota for using the gym equipment and discuss how things might be organized differently at home.

Answer [   ]

A practice situational awareness and problem solving test

If you find these questions easy when you have as much time as you like to decide on the right answer, then be careful that you do not run out of time in the real test before you have answered all the questions. In the real situation awareness test you have a little over one minute to answer each question so use the following 20 practice questions to identify the correct response when under the pressure of time.

Allow yourself 20 minutes to attempt the following 20 questions.

Do not turn over the page until you are ready to begin.

Q1 Your team is attending an incident at a block of flats and someone is calling for help from the very top storey. You and a colleague are told to take the stairs and investigate. Halfway up your colleague badly twists his ankle. He is in pain and cannot go any further. Would you:

A. Remain with your colleague until assistance arrives.

B. Return to the ground, helping your colleague.

C. Leave your colleague and continue alone to investigate.

D. Leave your colleague and return to get help.

Answer [　　　　　　　]

Q2 Your team has been called to tackle a fire that you are told has been deliberately lit. It is the third incident of arson in the area in less than two weeks. You arrive to see a group of youths running from the scene. Should you:

A. Give chase and apprehend them until the police arrive.

B. Tackle the fire.

C. Put out the fire and then go to see if you can find the youths.

D. Wait until the end of your shift and then go and see if you can find the perpetrators.

Answer [　　　　　　　]

Q3 Your team of seven is helping to evacuate an underground station. There is a thick, acrid smoke and it is critical that the large number of people there are got to the surface and fresh air as soon as possible. About a dozen people need to be carried and one of them is very large and too heavy for you to carry alone. Would you:

A. Help one of the other people to the surface and leave the heavy person behind.

B. Wait for a colleague to arrive and safely carry the person together.

C. Ask another of your team to try to carry the person.

D. Drag the person up the stairs even if it means their legs and feet get knocked and bruised.

Answer [　　　　　　　]

Q4 You realize that what was meant to have been a harmless bit of humour in fact upset someone. Would you:

A. Tell them that they should not be so sensitive.

B. Discuss it with your other colleagues when the person was not around.

C. Resolve never to do it again.

D. Apologize.

Answer

Q5 The senior firefighter at an incident sends you and a colleague into a burning property even though he knows there are canisters of propane gas stored there and they will explode if the fire reaches them. You have a young family to support. Would you:

A. Carry out the instruction.

B. Tell him that you will not go because you want to see your kids again.

C. Suggest he sends a member of the team with no family commitments instead of you.

D. Suggest your colleague goes alone rather than risk two lives.

Answer

Q6 You have been asked to complete a task before the end of your shift but it looks as if the job will take longer to complete than there is time left. Would you:

A. Stay late and finish the job.

B. Ask a colleague if he or she can spare the time to help you finish before the end of the shift.

C. Speed up to get the job done even if it means doing a less than perfect job.

D. Leave the job unfinished until you return on your next shift.

Answer

Q7   A bomb has already gone off around the corner. You are evacuating a building close to a suspect package and a member of the public is blocking the exit, refusing to allow anyone out of the building. Would you:

A.   Reason with him and explain the urgency of the situation.
B.   Insist that he moves aside so that others can leave the building.
C.   Pick him up and carry him out of the way.
D.   Order him to move and if he does not, physically remove him.

Answer ☐

Q8   You have been asked to find a senior officer and tell him something imperative. When you find him he is deep in conversation with another senior member of staff. Would you:

A.   Wait for a suitable pause in their conversation before you interrupt them.
B.   Stand nearby until they notice you and ask you what you want.
C.   Butt in immediately.
D.   Go back and tell them that you have found the officer but that he is in deep conversation.

Answer ☐

Q9   A vehicle is now well ablaze and the officer in charge calls your team back as the petrol tank could catch fire any moment. The elderly couple who were occupants of the car are very upset. You approach to comfort them and you are surprised to hear them plead that you rescue their cat, which is in a travel cage and still in the vehicle. Would you:

A.   Inform the officer in charge that a cat is in the car.
B.   Return to the car to rescue the cat.
C.   Tell them it is too late to help the cat.
D.   Say how sorry you are and explain that it is too dangerous to return to the vehicle.

Answer ☐

Q10 You have tried hard not to let it happen but problems in your personal life have been affecting your work recently, and it comes as no real surprise when your line manager takes you aside and says that she has noticed you seem distracted and are finding it hard to concentrate. She asks if there is anything the matter and if there is anything she could do to help. In such a situation would you:

A. Admit that there is a problem and tell her in broad terms what it involved.

B. Thank her for the concern, deny that there is a problem and resolve to try harder to keep your private and work life separate.

C. Politely point out that your private life is your own business and that you are not prepared to discuss it.

D. Apologize and say that you will try harder in the future.

Answer [   ]

Q11 On the way to an emergency you find the way blocked by a locked, unattended car that has been double parked. A detour would add considerably to your response time. Would you:

A. Ram it with the fire engine at speed to get through.

B. Slowly push the car out of the way with the fire engine.

C. Reverse the fire engine and take the detour to the emergency.

D. Disembark and between you bounce the car out of the way.

Answer [   ]

Q12 You notice that racist graffiti has been daubed across a hoarding next to the fire station. Would you:

A. Shake your head and say to yourself that people who do that kind of thing should be ashamed of themselves.

B. Put it on the agenda to be discussed at the next team meeting.

C. Immediately get a bucket and scrubbing brush and remove it.

D. Find out who owns the hoarding and telephone them asking them to get it removed as soon as possible.

Answer [   ]

Q13 You have been feeling unwell all day and nearly reported in sick but decided to go in to do your shift anyway. You are now feeling even worse; you feel weak and light-headed, and are finding it hard to concentrate. At that moment an emergency sounds and everyone is running to the vehicle. Should you:

A. Get on with it and ignore how you feel.

B. Join them and tell the officer in charge as soon as it is practical to do so.

C. Interrupt the preparations and tell the officer in charge about how you feel.

D. Stay behind to get some sleep to see if that improves things.

Answer [   ]

Q14 A delegation of community elders has arrived at the station to be shown around and to hold a discussion about how fire safety can be better promoted. You are answering their questions about your work when the call to an emergency sounds. Would you:

A. Avoid offence and finish the discussion before leaving the group to join the response team.

B. Risk offending them by apologizing and leaving immediately.

C. Not even waste time apologizing but simply turn and run to the response vehicle.

D. Leave the emergency to others and get on with the important work of community relations and fire safety.

Answer ☐

Q15 You undertake a formal visit to a business and discover in the storeroom a large quantity of highly inflammable material. The business does not have a fire certificate, as is required by law when such material is stored. Would you:

A. Call the police.

B. Warn the proprietor that he had better get it sorted before your next visit.

C. Immediately report your find to your line manager.

D. Remove the material and take it directly to the fire station.

Answer ☐

Q16 By chance you were on duty when a sales representative for low-consumption, long-life light bulbs called at the station. He offered to supply enough bulbs for the whole station at a special price or to invoice for a trial box of bulbs, again at an introductory low price. You had often thought that the fire station should do more to save energy and use such a product, so would you:

A. Show initiative and agree to the purchase of a trial box.

B. Be proactive and agree to the purchase of enough bulbs for the whole station and fit them yourself.

C. Explain that it is nothing to do with you and suggest he leaves the station.

D. Take details of the product and notify the appropriate member of staff.

Answer [   ]

Q17 You have just started two weeks of leave and your child's youth-club leader has asked you if a fire engine can be brought to the club one evening to promote fire safety. You think it is a brilliant opportunity because last year there were a number of accidents caused by youths misusing fireworks. Firework night is in one month's time. Should you:

A. Raise the opportunity when you return to work in two weeks' time.

B. Call your manager at home that evening to inform him of the invitation.

C. Say there may not be enough time to organize something this year but perhaps it can be sorted for next year.

D. Phone the station the next day and inform the duty manager of the opportunity.

Answer [   ]

Q18 It is night and you are called to an incident involving two vehicles known to be carrying toxic liquids. You are wearing a full protection suit and are told to cautiously investigate the scene. You see a liquid pouring from a tap on one of the vehicles. Should you:

A. Radio your find to the senior officer present and await instructions.

B. Get yourself out of there and report your find.

C. Try to turn the tap off to stop the flow and then report your actions.

D. Note your find and continue your investigation of the scene.

Answer [   ]

Q19 With the support of the police and staff from the ambulance service, your team is frantically working to extract a badly injured person at a road traffic accident. To everyone's horror another accident occurs on the other carriageway. It seems equally serious as cars are colliding into one another, and has been caused no doubt by drivers looking to see what you were doing rather than concentrating on the road ahead. Should you:

A. Get on with the extraction and not allow the other incident to distract you.

B. Stop what you are doing and go to see if anyone is injured.

C. Send one person from your team to investigate the other incident.

D. Move the fire engine so that it blocks the oncoming traffic's view of the incident.

Answer [   ]

Q20   You join a new team and are surprised to hear your new colleagues making homophobic remarks towards the youngest member of the team. Should you:

A.   Join in so that they more readily accept you into the team.

B.   Do nothing – after all it has probably been going on for a long time.

C.   Show your disagreement by not making the remarks yourself.

D.   Tell your new colleagues that you think it should stop.

Answer [   ]

Tests of observation

If you apply to one of the authorities still using the original national tests, then you may face a test of observation. These tests involve watching a short video and, once it has finished, answering a series of questions about it. You may have to watch a series of short video clips and answer questions after each one.

It helps if you can take notes during the video. The briefing before the video begins may well give an indication of what to look out for. Some of the videos lend themselves to your drawing a map and making notes at the points at which you see particular items. It is important that you are able to make notes while still watching, otherwise you risk missing important details while writing or drawing.

A useful tip is to devise suitable abbreviations beforehand. Using these can save you a lot of time when taking notes. They can also help avoid the problem that you cannot remember what your note stood for once you start answering the questions. For example, if you see two brown bags it is far quicker to write '2bb', but you need to take care that you remember that 'bb' stood for brown bag as it could also mean black box or blue bin. So decide in advance on convenient, unique abbreviations and stick to them while note taking.

Equipment assembling tests

Under the new structure of the national standards you are required to assemble a piece of equipment following written and illustrated instructions. To practise for this test, consider purchasing from a toyshop a number of the new LEGO kits. These comprise many small pieces and illustrated instructions that you must follow to assemble the toy. They are available at differing levels of complexity.

Fault diagnosis

For many practically orientated jobs the written test includes a fault diagnostic paper. A number of applicant firefighters have written to me requesting sources of practice for a fault diagnostic paper.

Normally we think of fault diagnosis as something that, for example, an electronic technician or an automobile technician would undertake to repair a computer or car. Obviously a technician brings a great deal of experience and specialist knowledge to the task of finding faults and repairing them, but in a fault diagnosis test no specialist knowledge is required.

Fault diagnosis tests investigate your ability to identify faults or errors in what are described as logical systems. By logical systems, the test author means a set of rules and an application of those rules. It is your task to say if there is a fault (error) in the application and if so where. This is not as complicated as it at might at first sound. Consider the following example of a logical system/set of rules:

Example 1

Logical system/rules

AB   Delete the last item

BC   Replace the third character with the next letter in the alphabet

CD   Insert the letter P between the fourth and fifth character.

DE   Exchange the first and last character.

The fault diagnostic question might start by stating a sequence of letters or numbers for example: OCTOBER. Next, some of the rules are applied to the opening sequence and the effect of the rule shown. For example:

Q1   OCTOBER → AB (delete the last item) = OCTOBE → CD (insert the letter P between the fourth and fifth character) = OCTOPBE

It is your task to judge whether the rules have been correctly applied and, if there is a fault, to identify at which point in the process it occurred. In this example there is no fault in the application of the rules. Normally the questions only contain the code for the rule.

Practice for fault diagnostic tests

The following 10 questions will help you prepare for a fault diagnostic test. They involve two sets of rules each followed by five questions. These questions are typically called input-type tests, and in fact a fault diagnostic test is a modified input-type test. Note that the task you are set in these 10 questions is to find the CORRECT application of the rules, not where a fault occurs. Despite this difference it is still good practice. You will find 100 practice input-type questions in the Kogan Page title *How to Pass Diagrammatic Reasoning Tests*, from where these 10 examples are taken. If you google 'fault diagnosis test' you will find a pdf download containing a fault diagnosis practice paper provided at: www.psychometric-success.com

Ten input-type questions

In the following 10 examples you must identify which of the suggested answers is the correct application of the logical system/rules.

Rules Q1–5:

AB   Delete the last character
BC   Replace the third character with the next in the alphabet
CD   Insert the letter P between the third and fourth characters
DE   Exchange the first and last characters
EF   Replace the second character with the previous letter in the alphabet
FG   Replace the fifth character with the next in the alphabet
GH   Reverse the whole sequence of letters
HI   Delete the third character

Q1 MOZLUCK → AB + FG + CD →   (A) MOZPLVK

(B) MOZLVC

(C) MOZPLVCK

(D) MOZPLVC

Answer

Q2 CNPTTBM → HI + EF + DE →   (A) MMTTBC

(B) MMTTBM

(C) MNTTBC

(D) CMTTBC

Answer

Q3 GUAGEDR → BC + GH + FG →   (A) GUBGEDR

(B) DDGECUG

(C) RDEGCUG

(D) RDGEBUG

Answer

Q4 PBSATTS → HI + CD + EF →   (A) PBSPATTS

(B) PBAPUTS

(C) PBPATTS

(D) PBSAPTT

Answer

Q5 NOITIDE → AB + FG + GH →   (A) DITTON

(B) DITION

(C) DJTION

(D) EDITION

Answer

Rules Q6–10:

◼ Cancel all shading

◯ Shade the second and last shapes

● Exchange the second and fourth shapes

▢ Reverse the sequence of shapes

⬇ Change all circles to shaded squares

⇩ Replace all shaded shapes with unshaded triangles (with the apex at the top)

▲ Replace the first shape with a shaded triangle with its apex pointing downwards

△ Change the middle shape to an unshaded circle

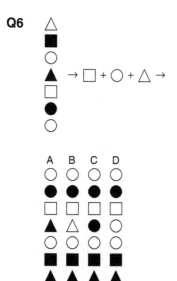

Q6

Answer [   ]

Rules Q6–10:

■ Cancel all shading

◯ Shade the second and last shapes

● Exchange the second and fourth shapes

☐ Reverse the sequence of shapes

⬇ Change all circles to shaded squares

⇩ Replace all shaded shapes with unshaded triangles (with the apex at the top)

▲ Replace the first shape with a shaded triangle with its apex pointing downwards

△ Change the middle shape to an unshaded circle

Q7

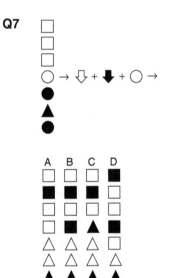

Answer [   ]

Q8

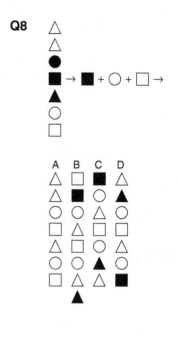

Answer [   ]

Q9

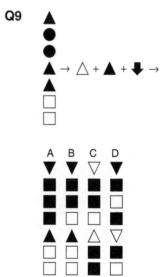

Answer [   ]

Rules Q6–10:

■ Cancel all shading

○ Shade the second and last shapes

● Exchange the second and fourth shapes

▢ Reverse the sequence of shapes

⬇ Change all circles to shaded squares

⇩ Replace all shaded shapes with unshaded triangles (with the apex at the top)

▼ Replace the first shape with a shaded triangle with its apex pointing downwards

△ Change the middle shape to an unshaded circle

Q10

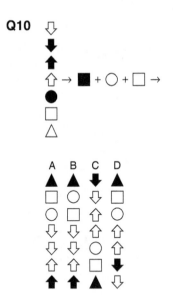

Answer [   ]

Spatial recognition and visual estimation

Below you will find practice for three types of spatial or visual estimation tests. In the first example your task is to identify the plan of a three-dimensional shape. A plan is the view of the shape looking exactly down. In the second type you have to identify the shape that has been rotated but is otherwise identical to the question shape (all the others would have been rotated but changed in some way too). In the last type of question you must identify the shape that could be contrasted if the two example shapes are combined. No other change should be made to the shapes other than combining them.

You will find 100 practice questions for spatial recognition and visual estimation in the title *How to Pass Diagrammatic Reasoning Tests* published by Kogan Page, from where these 15 examples have been taken.

Type 1

Identify the plan of the three-dimensional shape in the following five questions.

Q1

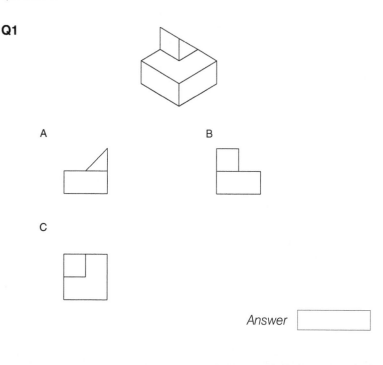

A

B

C

Answer

Q2

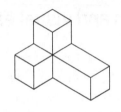

A

B

C

Answer

Q3

A

B

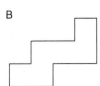

C

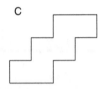

Answer

Q4

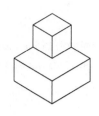

A

B

C

Answer

Q5

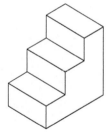

A

B

C

Answer

Type 2

Identify the shape that has been rotated but is otherwise identical to the questions' shape in the following five questions.

Q6

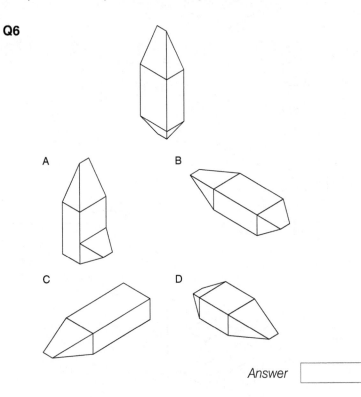

A

B

C

D

Answer

Q7

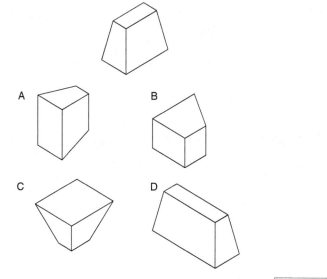

Answer

Q8

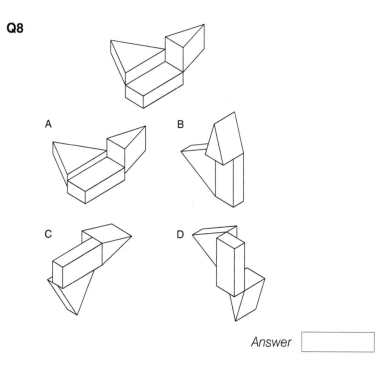

Answer

Q9

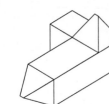

A 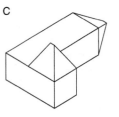   B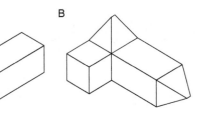

C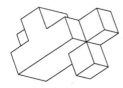

Answer

Q10

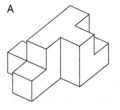

A 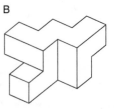   B

C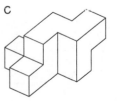

Answer

Type 3

Identify the new shape that could be constructed if the two example shapes were combined in the following five questions.

Q11

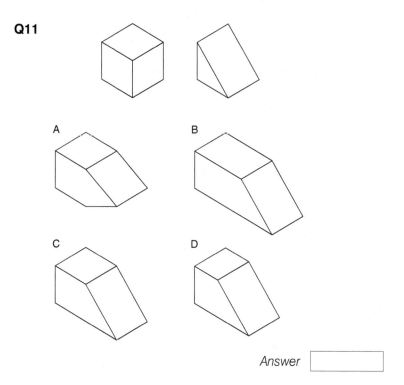

A

B

C

D

Answer [   ]

Q12

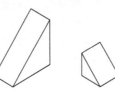

A   B

C   D

Answer

Q13

A   B

C   D

Answer

Q14

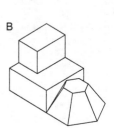

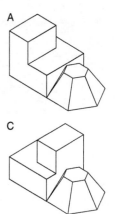

Answer

Q15

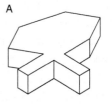

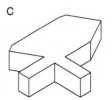

Answer

CHAPTER 4

Practice tests

This chapter comprises three realistic practice tests. Use them to develop a test strategy for winning under the pressure of time.

To get the most from these practice tests you should try to create as realistic a test situation as possible. Work in a quiet place without interruption and be strict about stopping when you have used up all the time allowed. Use the last few minutes to attempt all remaining questions.

If you run out of time before you have attempted all the questions, then you need to increase the speed at which you work and not fall into the trap of spending too long on any one question.

Realize that to do well in a test you really have to try hard and you should, when the test is finished, feel exhausted from the exertion. If you do not, then you have probably not applied yourself sufficiently.

If you hit a string of questions to which you do not know the answers then keep going. You may find the next set of questions far more approachable.

Make sure that you pay attention to how many questions you have attempted. In some of the tests, at the bottom of each page you are told to turn over the page. This means that there are more questions to go.

Answers and many explanations are found in Chapter 6.

Practice test 1: understanding information

Read each passage and answer the questions that follow. There are six passages, each followed by five questions.

You have 12 minutes in which to attempt all 30 questions.

Only refer to information provided in the passage to answer the questions.

Work quickly and indicate which of the suggested answers you consider correct.

Please note that the content of the passages is intended only to provide realistic test practice. They do not necessarily report what you should do if a fire occurs or accurately describe the responsibilities of employers or the fire authorities.

Should you wish to obtain such advice, then contact your local fire station or visit sites such as www.firekills-gov.uk/.

Do not turn the page until you are ready to begin.

Passage 1

We can all recognize fire but the majority of us fail to fully understand it. Once started, a fire may grow unexpectedly fast and in very little time it can threaten life and property. The potential for an accidental fire exists in a large number of everyday activities, including driving a car, cooking, using electrical equipment and working.

Every year people are killed, and even more are injured, by fires that occur in the workplace, whilst travelling and in the home. The cost of a fire in terms of the loss of possessions and interruption to business can be equally devastating. The cost to business through fire runs to many millions of pounds every year and some companies fail to recover from its effects.

Q1   If a fire occurs a business:

    A.   May cost many millions of pounds.

    B.   May lose many millions of pounds.

    C.   May not recover from it.

    D.   Is unlikely to recover from it.

Answer [   ]

Q2   Once fires start they can:

    A.   Grow at an alarming rate.

    B.   Burn away unnoticed.

    C.   Generate lots of smoke.

    D.   Overcome people with the heat they produce.

Answer [   ]

Q3   The passage specifically states that there is a risk of an accidental fire occurring when:

    A.   Smoking in bed.

    B.   Operating equipment at work.

    C.   Driving a car.

    D.   Deep-fat frying.

Answer [   ]

Q4 While most people do not fully understand fire:

A. Firefighters, because of their training, do.

B. The majority can identify it.

C. They know that they should call the Fire Service if it occurs.

D. They can all recognize it.

Answer [   ]

Q5 More people:

A. Are injured in accidental fires at work than at home or while travelling.

B. Are injured in accidental fires at work, home and while travelling than are killed by them.

C. Die in accidental fires while travelling than at home and work.

D. Die in accidental fires at work, home and while travelling than are injured by them.

Answer [   ]

Passage 2

Every business should ensure that employees know what to do in the event of a fire. Time must also be taken to ensure that staff know how to prevent accidental fires in the first place. These simple precautions could save a business from having to face the devastating effects of an accidental fire, and for this reason alone taking such precautions makes sound business sense. However, the law also compels most employers to provide adequate training in fire awareness and fire safety for all members of their staff. The United Kingdom's fire authorities are recognized throughout the world as a leading voice in fire safety. They have earned this recognition because of the many decades of experience they have had and because their workforce is trained to the very highest standards.

Q6 Complying with the law is:

    A. Not the main reason why an employer should ensure that staff know what to do in the event of a fire.

    B. The main reason why an employer should ensure that staff know what to do in the event of a fire.

    C. The only reason why an employer should ensure that staff know what to do in the event of a fire.

    D. Is not a reason why an employer should ensure that staff know what to do in the event of a fire.

Answer ▢

Q7 Which of the following is true?

    A. Just a few simple safety measures could save a business from having to face the devastating effects of an accidental fire.

    B. Simple safety measures could save a business from having to face the devastating effects of an accidental fire.

    C. A number of impractical precautions could save a business from having to face the devastating effects of an accidental fire.

    D. A number of unspecified precautions could save a business from having to face the devastating effects of an accidental fire.

Answer ▢

Q8 The law requires that adequate training in fire awareness be provided by:

    A. Every large employer.

    B. Most employers.

    C. Some employers.

    D. All employers.

Answer ▢

Q9   The UK's fire authorities:

A. Operate in the UK only.

B. Train all their staff in fire safety.

C. Employ a large number of highly trained staff.

D. Have staff trained to a very high standard.

Answer ☐

Q10   Employers:

A. Can be prosecuted if they fail to provide fire-safety training to their staff.

B. Should be prosecuted if they fail to provide fire-safety training to their staff.

C. Should provide fire-safety training to their staff.

D. Can provide fire-safety training to their staff.

Answer ☐

Passage 3

Many fires in the home start at night when the occupants are asleep. Everyone should follow a fire-safety routine before going to bed. Such a routine involves switching off and unplugging any electrical appliance that is not designed to stay on. So switch off and unplug everything other than, for example, the video and fridge. If anyone smokes in the house, make sure that any cigarettes are extinguished and that the contents of ashtrays are cold. Discourage anyone in the household from smoking in bed. If you have an open fire, let it burn well down before you go to bed and always use a spark guard. Do not be tempted to run a washing machine at night as these can catch fire when operating and are not designed to stay on all the time. Close all doors throughout your property as this will slow down the spread of any heat or smoke generated by a fire. Practise such a routine every evening and your home will be considerably safer from the threat of a fire.

Q11   Accidental fires in the home:

   A.   Are more likely to start at night than during the day.
   B.   Are common at night.
   C.   Are more common at night.
   D.   Always start at night when the occupants are asleep.

Answer [ ]

Q12   You should unplug the:

   A.   Washing machine at night.
   B.   DVD player at night.
   C.   Fridge at night.
   D.   Table lamp at night.

Answer [ ]

Q13   Open fires should:

   A.   Be in a room where the door is closed.
   B.   Have a guard in front of them at night.
   C.   Be discouraged in a house.
   D.   Have a guard in front of them in order to stop sparks.

Answer [ ]

Q14   The advice to follow a fire-safety routine:

   A.   Does not apply to people who live alone.
   B.   Applies to people who smoke.
   C.   Does not apply to people who live with others.
   D.   Applies to everybody.

Answer [ ]

Q15   Heat and smoke generated by a fire can spread through a house. Closing doors:

   A.   Stops this from happening.
   B.   Helps this effect.
   C.   Helps slow down this effect.
   D.   Does not stop this.

Answer [ ]

Passage 4

Fit a smoke alarm in your home and it could save your life. If you already have a smoke alarm then make sure that it is operational by testing it. Regularly check that the battery is not flat, otherwise it will fail to warn you should a fire occur.

You can buy smoke alarms for under £5 from a DIY, electrical or hardware shop. Some garages and supermarkets also sell them. Fit a smoke alarm between your living area and the bedrooms. Ideally, you should also fit one in every room except the bedrooms. Make sure that you can hear it throughout your home, especially in the bedrooms. Test it each month by pressing the test button. Change the battery every year. From time to time, use a vacuum cleaner to get rid of any dust inside.

If the low battery warning sounds (usually an intermittent bleep), replace the battery with a new one. If you have difficulty in hearing, then you can buy a smoke alarm that has a vibrating pad or flashing light. Further information on these products can be obtained from the Royal National Institute for the Deaf or from your local fire station. Remember that a smoke alarm is useless if it does not have a battery or if the battery is flat.

Q16   Smoke alarms are:

    A.   Not suitable for people who have difficulty with hearing.
    B.   Ineffective without a battery.
    C.   Not available in garages.
    D.   Cheapest in supermarkets.

Answer [   ]

Q17   Ideally you should fit a smoke alarm:

    A.   In every room with the exception of the bedrooms.
    B.   In every room.
    C.   In every room especially the bedrooms.
    D.   Between your living room and bedrooms.

Answer [   ]

(Turn over the page)

Q18 The passage states that you should test a smoke alarm every month and:

    A. Vacuum it to remove dust once a year.
    B. Vacuum it to remove dust.
    C. Vacuum it to remove dust from time to time.
    D. Vacuum it to remove dust every month or two.

Answer

Q19 Special smoke alarms are available for people:

    A. Who smoke.
    B. With lots of money.
    C. Who can't afford one.
    D. With a disability.

Answer

Q20 The main point of the passage is to provide:

    A. A conclusion drawn from facts regarding fire safety.
    B. Advice that, if followed, could save lives.
    C. The case for and against fitting a smoke alarm.
    D. Warnings about the risks of not having a working smoke alarm in your home.

Answer

Passage 5

Most employers are required by law under the Fire Precautions Workplace Regulations 1997 to carry out a fire risk assessment and record the findings of that assessment. They must also provide and maintain precautions to keep people safe from fire in the workplace and give information, instructions and training to staff about these fire precautions. They must also have a written fire emergency plan.

Fire authorities are responsible for the supervision and enforcement of the regulations. A fire-safety inspecting officer can prohibit the use of a part or all of a building with immediate effect if he or she thinks it is unsafe. Officers can also issue an enforcement notice requiring improvements to be made. Failure of an employer to comply with the regulations is a criminal act and the fire authorities may prosecute in the courts.

Q21   Employers must record:

A. Their fire risk assessment.

B. When they undertook a fire risk assessment.

C. Who undertook the fire risk assessment.

D. The conclusions of their fire risk assessment.

Answer [   ]

Q22   A written fire emergency plan is something that by law:

A. All employers must have.

B. Most employers must have.

C. Employers may choose to have.

D. Very few employers need to have.

Answer [   ]

Q23   A fire-safety inspecting officer can:

A. Prosecute in the courts.

B. Not stop people from working in a part of a building if he or she considers it unsafe.

C. Stop people from working in a part of a building if he or she considers it unsafe.

D. Not prosecute in the courts.

Answer [   ]

Q24   Fire authorities are responsible for:

A. Prosecutions, although this would be the last resort.

B. Supervision and enforcement of the regulations.

C. Supervision of the regulations.

D. Enforcement of the regulations; fire-safety inspecting officers are responsible for the supervision.

Answer [   ]

(Turn over the page)

Q25   A word or phrase that means the same as supervision is:

    A.   Management.

    B.   Good eyesight.

    C.   Enforcement.

    D.   Greater than.

                             Answer

Passage 6

As well as complying with the fire regulations, some premises also require a fire certificate. These are legal documents that set out the fire precautionary arrangements of the building. Fire certificates are required if the premises are hotels or boarding houses that provide sleeping accommodation for six or more people, or if sleeping accommodation is provided above the first floor or below ground level. Factories, shops, offices and railway stations where more than 20 people work at any one time must also obtain certificates. Any site at which explosive or highly flammable material is stored must also obtain a fire certificate.

Q26   A fire certificate is required by:

    A.   A two-storey hotel with accommodation for four people.

    B.   A three-storey hotel with accommodation for five people.

    C.   A hotel with accommodation for six people.

    D.   An office.

                             Answer

Q27   A railway station where 20 people work:

    A.   Would require a fire certificate.

    B.   Would not require a fire certificate.

    C.   Might well require a fire certificate.

    D.   Might not require a fire certificate.

                             Answer

Q28 A warehouse containing fireworks that employs only a night watchman:

A. Does not require a fire certificate.
B. Requires a fire certificate.
C. Might require a fire certificate.
D. May not require a fire certificate.

Answer [   ]

Q29 A large shop in which 30 people work but not all at the same time:

A. Requires a fire certificate.
B. Does not require a fire certificate.
C. Might not require a fire certificate.
D. May not require a fire certificate.

Answer [   ]

Q30 If an employer has a fire certificate for their premises then:

A. They must also comply with the fire regulations.
B. They must comply either with the fire regulations or with the conditions stated in the fire certificate.
C. They automatically comply with the fire regulations (otherwise the fire certificate would not have been issued).
D. They do not have to comply with the fire regulations.

Answer [   ]

End of test.

Practice test 2: using numbers and time

Quick 25-question test

This test comprises 25 questions that test your command of the key skills examined by real firefighter tests.

Allow yourself 13 minutes in which to complete the test. Really go for it and do not stop until you run out of time.

You will need to work as quickly as possible.

Do not use a calculator.

Do not turn the page until you are ready to begin.

Q1   The time now is 12.16. What was the time 55 minutes ago?

Answer [   ]

Q2   The time now is 03.40. What was the time 2 hours and 16 minutes ago?

Answer [   ]

Q3   The time now is 04.07. What was the time 33 minutes ago?

Answer [   ]

Q4   The time now is 12.03. What was the time 1 hour 47 minutes ago?

Answer [   ]

Q5   If the time now is 06.21, what was the time 51 minutes ago?

Answer [   ]

Q6   An emergency call was logged at 21.00 hours and the time now is 22.17. How many minutes have passed since the emergency call was logged?

Answer [   ]

Q7   If a block of flats contains 24 dwellings, four on each floor, how many storeys high is the block?

Answer [   ]

Q8   Your colleagues responded to an emergency 50 minutes ago. The time now is 04.23. What was the time when the response began?

Answer [   ]

Q9   If one in three households does not have a working smoke alarm, how many homes are unprotected in a town of 2,100 homes?

Answer

Q10   If you entered a smoke-filled house at 09.41 and the time is now 10.13, how long have you been in the building?

Answer

Q11   320 people were present in a building when the practice evacuation took place. The fire marshal reported 281 people assembled at the meeting place. How many people were unaccounted for?

Answer

Q12   If a burning vehicle is reported at 12.44 and the emergency services arrive at the scene at 13.12, how long was the interval between the report and the arrival of the emergency services?

Answer

Q13   One in five calls to the emergency services are hoax calls; if a fire station receives 30 calls a week, how many are likely to be hoaxes?

Answer

Q14   If the time now is 13.52, what will be the time in 37 minutes?

Answer

Q15   If a block of flats comprises nine floors, each with three flats, how many flats are there in the block?

Answer

(Turn over the page)

Q16 If an emergency call was made at 01.13 and it took 25 minutes for the fire crew to reach the location of the emergency, what was the time when the fire crew arrived at the scene?

Answer [ ]

Q17 If two in five households include at least one person who smokes, how many homes from a total of 200 include one smoker or more?

Answer [ ]

Q18 Three hours and 20 minutes is how many minutes?

Answer [ ]

Q19 In an incident, 13 people were reported missing while 297 were accounted for. What is the total count of people involved?

Answer [ ]

Q20 An emergency call was logged at 09.21 and the time now is 10.07. How many minutes have passed since the emergency call was logged?

Answer [ ]

Q21 One in four calls to the emergency service are fire-related. If a total of 280 calls are received, how many would you expect to be fire-related?

Answer [ ]

Q22 Your colleagues responded to an emergency 70 minutes ago, and the time now is 01.15. What was the time when the response began?

Answer [ ]

Q23 To stay fit a firefighter went on a 2-km run, three times a week. How many kilometres did she run in a six-week period?

Answer [   ]

Q24 If you entered a smoke-filled room at 03.11 and the time is now 04.03, how long have you been in the building?

Answer [   ]

Q25 In a 50-hour period of duty, a watch was out responding to emergencies 12 per cent of the time. For how much time was the watch not out responding to emergencies?

Answer [   ]

End of test.

Practice test 3: listening to information

Instructions

In your real exam to become a firefighter, you may face a test that requires you to listen to an audio passage and then answer questions. These practice questions will give you a real sense of what to expect and allow you to develop a winning approach.

To benefit from this practice, however, you will need someone's help. You will need to get someone to read the passages to you and then you can answer the questions.

Do not read the passages yourself – you need to practise listening and remembering as these are the skills examined in the test.

You do not need to set a time limit, because the longer you take the harder it gets to remember what you heard. Try taking notes but be careful that you do not miss the next bit of information while you write. Some people find it useful to leave any question that they cannot immediately answer to last.

Each passage is on a separate page and the questions are over the page.

Remember that to get the most out of this practice you should not read the passages yourself.

Do not turn the page until you are ready to begin.

Note to the passage reader

Read each passage only once at a slow and steady rate. Advise when you are about to start and when the passage is finished. Then instruct the test taker to turn over the page and begin the questions. Do not allow them to read the passage, nor should they see the questions until after they have heard the passage. If they wish they may take notes on a separate piece of paper.

Passage 1

Youngsters setting fire to rubbish and misusing fireworks in the Southfield area of Newbury are endangering their own and others' lives. A fire appliance and crew will visit the area on Sunday and the firefighters will try to talk to the young people about fire safety.

The police will be visiting local traders to discourage them from selling fireworks to anyone under the age of 18. They will be visiting the parents of young offenders and arresting anyone found to be throwing fireworks, lighting fires or engaging in any other sort of dangerous behaviour.

Officers and firefighters are very concerned that someone could end up hurt. Every year over 543 people in the age range 16 to 18 are seriously injured by fireworks.

Q1   Southfield is in Newport.

True
False
Cannot say

Answer [   ]

Q2   The fire appliance is due to visit the area on Saturday.

True
False
Cannot say

Answer [   ]

Q3   Over 500 people a year aged 16 to 18 are injured by fireworks.

True
False
Cannot say

Answer [   ]

Q4   Local traders have been selling fireworks to the youngsters.

    True
    False
    Cannot say

                             Answer [   ]

Q5   Someone has already been hurt by the youngsters' behaviour.

    True
    False
    Cannot say

                             Answer [   ]

Do not turn over the page until you have heard the next passage.

Passage 2

The Fire Service not only puts out fires but also works to ensure that they do not happen in the first place. Where there is the greatest risk of fires, the service will make the greatest effort to reduce that risk. The principal way in which the Fire Service will try to prevent fires is through raising awareness and understanding of fire-safety issues. The greatest efforts will be made to educate members of the public most likely to be the victims of fire, for example the elderly, those living alone and smokers.

Community fire-safety schemes will operate from fire stations and firefighters will spend time in the community advising, for example, employers on their fire-safety precautions and installing smoke alarms in the homes of members of the public who are at most risk of fire. Already over 13,000 smoke alarms, with batteries that last 10 years, have been fitted under this initiative. Fire stations will be open to the public, offering advice on fire and community safety. Wherever possible they will be made fully accessible to people with disabilities.

Q6 You can get a free smoke alarm from your local fire-safety scheme.

True
False
Cannot say

Answer

Q7 All fire stations will be open to the public.

True
False
Cannot say

Answer

Q8 The batteries in the smoke alarms have to be changed every year.

True
False
Cannot say

Answer

Q9 All fire stations will be made accessible to people with disabilities.

True
False
Cannot say

Answer

Q10 13,000 smoke alarms have already been fitted by the Fire Service.

True
False
Cannot say

Answer

Do not turn over the page until you have heard the next passage.

Passage 3

Over a five-year period 418 people died in fires in London, and an analysis of those tragic deaths found that those at most risk of dying in a fire in their home were people over 60 years of age who live alone, smoke and drink, and do not have an operational smoke alarm. It was also found that people living in three of the London boroughs were more at risk.

Over half of the accidental fire deaths in the home were caused by smoking or matches; cooking was the next most common cause, giving rise to almost 20 per cent of the deaths, followed by candles, which caused a further 10 per cent of the tragedies.

Alcohol was found to have played a role in a third of the fatal accidents, and men were more likely than women to be victims of such an accident. It was also found that a higher proportion of deaths occurred in winter.

Q11 Smoking or matches caused over half of the accidental fire deaths in the home.

True
False
Cannot say

Answer [   ]

Q12 Residents of four London boroughs have a higher risk of dying in an accidental home fire.

True
False
Cannot say

Answer [   ]

Q13 In the winter months men are more likely to die in an accidental fire in the home.

True
False
Cannot say

Answer [   ]

Q14 Cooking causes almost 20 per cent of deaths from accidental home fires.

True
False
Cannot say

Answer [   ]

Q15 People who smoke and drink alcohol, who are aged over 60 and live alone are most at risk.

True
False
Cannot say

Answer [   ]

Do not turn over the page until you have heard the next passage.

Passage 4

Yorkshire firefighters taking part in the national extraction competition were awarded second place. The competition involves teams of firefighters from all over the country demonstrating their skills at cutting out and removing casualties from serious road traffic accidents.

The competitions are held every two years and teams are judged as they cut trapped dummies from a simulated two-car accident. They are allowed 20 minutes and must work with hydraulic tools and power-driven saws to extract the victims safely.

First place was awarded to a team from South Wales, and in total 30 teams took part.

It is believed that the competitions greatly improve the teams' skills in this challenging part of a firefighter's job and are invaluable in the real-life situations they face.

Q16   The competition is held annually.

True
False
Cannot say

Answer [   ]

Q17   The Yorkshire team came second.

True
False
Cannot say

Answer [   ]

Q18   The simulated accident involves two dummies.

True
False
Cannot say

Answer [   ]

Q19   The teams have 20 minutes in which to free the dummies.

True
False
Cannot say

Answer [   ]

Q20   The passage suggests that the competition is international.

True
False
Cannot say

Answer [   ]

Do not turn over the page until you have heard the next passage.

Passage 5

The most common sort of fire in the kitchen is caused by deep-fat frying. It is an accident that is shockingly common and 4,000 people are injured each year in the UK by this sort of fire.

These fires could all be avoided if people followed some basic rules when doing this sort of cooking. First of all, people must realize that they are doing something really quite dangerous – they are heating on average a litre of oil to a high temperature. This oil can cause serious burns if spilt and it can also catch fire. Once alight it is difficult to put out.

The safest way to deep fry is to use an electric deep fryer that has a fitted thermostat control to prevent the oil from overheating. If such a fryer is unavailable the risk of an accident can be reduced if people:

- do not fill the pan more than one-third full of oil;

- never leave the kitchen when they are deep-fat frying;

- turn the heat off if the oil begins to smoke and allow it to cool;

- only fry food that has been dried before it is put in the oil (water on the food could cause the oil to explode).

Q21 Deep-fat frying is dangerous.

True
False
Cannot say

Answer _____

Q22 The most common sort of fire is caused by deep-fat frying.

True
False
Cannot say

Answer _____

Q23 Water can cause the oil to explode.

True
False
Cannot say

Answer _____

Q24 The average quantity of oil used in a deep-fat fryer is 1 litre.

True
False
Cannot say

Answer _____

Q25 A pan should not be more than 33.3 per cent full.

True
False
Cannot say

Answer _____

Do not turn over the page until you have heard the next passage.

Passage 6

A simulated chemical attack on the London Underground took place so that the emergency services could practise dealing with a major incident of this kind. In the simulation, casualties had to wait half an hour for help to arrive. It took three hours before the last casualty was brought to street level.

The Commissioner of the Fire Brigade concluded that the emergency services would have to find ways in which they could more quickly reach victims of any future real attack. He felt this was bound to be one of the major lessons learnt from the exercise at Bank Station.

The exercise took place under the financial centre of the capital city and was intended to be as realistic as possible. The emergency service staff wore full gas-protection suits during the exercise and filled dummies were used as victims, each of which weighed 13 stone. However, the firefighters were not allowed to carry the dummies to the surface as the Health and Safety Executive felt that their weight represented too great a risk to the firefighters' health. The dummies were dragged to the surface instead.

Q26 It took over three hours before the last victim was brought to ground level.

True
False
Cannot say

Answer

Q27 The dummies weighed 13 stone.

True
False
Cannot say

Answer

Q28 The exercise was held in Euston Station.

True
False
Cannot say

Answer

Q29 It must have been hot working in the gas-protection suits.

True
False
Cannot say

Answer

Q30 It is fair to say that it took the emergency services longer than they expected to get to the victims.

True
False
Cannot say

Answer

Do not turn over the page until you have heard the next passage.

Passage 7

The White Paper *Our Fire and Rescue Service* sets out the government's strategy for achieving a modern fire and rescue service in England and Wales.

The report argues that the service must develop a broader role in the prevention of fires and be able to respond to a wider range of threats and hazards, thereby creating safer communities for us all.

The priorities of the service are stated as: working to prevent fires and, when they occur, saving lives and reducing injuries, and planning for emergencies and environmental disasters and the growing threat of terrorism.

Q31 The government's strategy is intended for the whole of Great Britain.

True
False
Cannot say

Answer [   ]

Q32 The role of the service must be widened.

True
False
Cannot say

Answer [   ]

Q33 The government's document was described in the passage as a Green Paper.

True
False
Cannot say

Answer [   ]

Q34 The growing threat of terrorism is one reason behind the changes posed in the passage.

True
False
Cannot say

Answer [   ]

Q35 The passage states the priorities of the fire and rescue service.

True
False
Cannot say

Answer [   ]

Do not turn over the page until you have heard the next passage.

Passage 8

The largest single cause of deaths and injuries from fire is accidental fires in the home. There is a growing trend in deliberate fires, up by 25 per cent since 1996. Those most likely to be at risk from fire, whether accidental or deliberately set, are the poorest in our society. They are more likely to have a fire in their home and they are less likely to be insured.

The Fire Service has a key role in the promotion of fire safety to encourage safe behaviour in all sections of our community and to work to reduce the incidents of arson.

Q36 Most accidental fires that lead to death or injury occur in the home.

True
False
Cannot say

Answer

Q37 Arson is on the increase.

True
False
Cannot say

Answer

Q38 The poorest in our community are more likely to deliberately start fires.

True
False
Cannot say

Answer

Q39 The only role of the Fire Service is to put out fires.

True
False
Cannot say

Answer

Q40 We can be proud of our Fire Service.

True
False
Cannot say

Answer

End of test.

CHAPTER 5

Interview and team exercise, physical tests and references

Congratulations if you are reading this chapter after being notified that you have passed the written tests and are invited to attend the next stage of the process. You have succeeded where many other very good candidates have failed.

Allow yourself a day or two to enjoy your achievement, but then put aside any sense of pride and start to take very seriously the remaining challenges. In a few weeks' time or possibly sooner, you must demonstrate that you are very well suited to the role of fire-fighter. There will be a lot of other candidates trying to do the same and there will not be enough positions for all of you. The recruiters will have to make some difficult decisions and will have to choose between candidates on the basis of what they say and how well they represent themselves on the day.

With your letter of notification you will receive information about the remaining assessments, and an address and map detailing when and where you must attend. It may be the same place that you attended for the written tests but this is not guaranteed, so check the address.

The administrators will want to be able to confirm that no one is impersonating you and attending on your behalf, so they are likely to require ID. Read carefully and follow the instructions on your invitation; if they require ID they will stipulate which form they accept. Contact them if you have any questions. They will also detail what you should take along, and this may include sports clothes in which to undertake the physical tests. It would be a big mistake to arrive late for your appointment, so locate the centre and make sure you can find it with time to spare. The day may well start early so plan your route, leaving plenty of time to arrive. It is very unlikely that you will be able to join if you arrive late. It may be a long day and by the end of it you may well be flagging, but first and foremost try to enjoy it!

The attendees will be divided into groups and each group will undertake the various assignments at different times. You may, for example, do the group exercise first followed by a physical test, while others do the physical test first.

Dress smartly but comfortably; guys, a suit and tie is not necessary but by all means wear one if you wish.

Note that a self-assessment form can figure as part of your assessment – so answer it thoughtfully and be self-critical, especially with respect to how you might improve your performance.

If you are asked to compete in a group exercise

What it involves

A group exercise involves you sitting with a group of other candidates and being observed and assessed and even possibly videotaped while you discuss a number of topics related to the Fire Service. These exercises can be organized in a number of ways but in general they involve each candidate taking it in turns to introduce a topic and then the whole group discussing it.

You will be given details of your subject a few minutes before the start of the exercise and you may use the remaining time to prepare what you wish to say and collect your thoughts. When the exercise begins, each candidate takes it in turns to introduce the subject and then open it up for discussion within the group. When it is your subject, you are leading the discussion. When it is the turn of other candidates to introduce their topics, it is your role to listen carefully and to make a contribution to the discussions that they lead.

In this sort of exercise the assessors are looking for candidates who can:

● have a constructive conversation with people they have not previously met;

● listen to the views of others;

● develop a view by incorporating the ideas of others;

● speak confidently and clearly on a subject that is new to them;

● encourage and support others in a conversation.

Make best use of the preparation time

During the preparation time, list points that you feel are important and you believe should make for a constructive, relevant discussion. Don't worry if someone raises one of your points before you get the chance to make it, just contribute to its discussion and help develop the issue. It is vital to listen to others. The selectors will be looking to see if your input helps to move the discussion forward, and whether you help the group to achieve its objectives.

Some people find they can better structure their ideas if they organize them using an assessment tool. Examples include SWOT and PEST (strengths/weaknesses/opportunities/threats, and political/economic/social/technological). Another commonly used tool is the spider diagram, which can help with recall. If you think such an approach would benefit you, then make sure you are familiar with using these tools beforehand. Consider the illustration below.

Example

In a group exercise two candidates are given the following topics to introduce for discussion: 'Improving disabled access' and 'Providing smoke detectors'. One decides to use the SWOT assessment tool to help structure the introduction; the other decides to use the PEST tool. Each makes notes in preparation for the presentation, as shown in the boxes below.

Topic 1

The Fire Service has decided to improve the disabled access to your fire station and you and a group of colleagues are charged with working out how these improvements could improve the service you provide.

Notes

- Strengths/Opportunities

  - More people who suffer disabilities could visit the station and so help raise awareness of the role of the Fire Service, and raise understanding of fire-safety issues within this group.

  - Firefighters would meet more people with disabilities and so better understand their needs.

- Weaknesses/Threats

  - People with disabilities have many different needs, and modifications may not succeed in providing access for everyone; should consult with disabled groups on what modifications to make.

  - Providing access alone may not be enough; also need to reach out to the disabled community through visits.

Topic 2

Money has been found to install smoke detectors in the homes of people judged to be most at risk of fire. You and some colleagues are charged with discussing how it would be best to implement this new initiative.

Notes

- Political/Social
  - Need to consider how to advertise the scheme so that people from ethnic minority groups and people who do not speak English access the service.
  - Many people will not be able to fit the alarm, so firefighters should offer to fit one for them.
- Economic/Technological
  - People most at risk need alarms with very long battery life and very low or no maintenance requirements as they may not be able to afford replacement batteries or undertake maintenance.
  - Should consider combined detectors that sense carbon monoxide as well as smoke.
  - Need to consider needs of people with poor hearing or vision and provide detectors adapted for their needs.

Make a winning impression

When it comes to the actual exercise, try to forget that you are being observed and focus your attention on the group, its objective and the discussion. Lift your head up high, introduce yourself to the group in a clear, confident voice and be sure to make lots of eye contact. Do nod in agreement but don't shake your head or demonstrate disagreement through body language. Don't worry if the position you adopt during a discussion is entirely different from everyone else's. The selectors are assessing how well you can make your case rather than analysing the case that you are making.

Demonstrate that you can listen and have understood the significance of contributions by others in the group by making explicative reference to how you have modified your case. Do this by, for example, offering brief supportive summaries of their contributions and then adding a further relevant point of your own.

Set out to make as good a case as you can for the view that you are representing. Do not take criticism personally and don't start or get sucked into an argument. In the unlikely event that one occurs, do try to help make peace between the parties. Make sure you are enthusiastic even when discussing what might seem to be very mundane issues.

Keep your contributions to the point and spell out the relevance if you refer to something not obviously significant to the issue under discussion. Always be constructive in your contributions and be supportive of others in your group.

It is better to avoid taking notes during the exercise. If you really must take them, keep them extremely brief. One-word notes are best, as you really do not want the invigilators to see you looking down. You want them to notice lots of eye contact and nods in agreement, showing that you can listen and have understood the significance of the contribution of others.

Be very careful not to stray into language that could be taken as aggressive. Listen as well as talk. Use 'us' and 'we' to emphasize the collective. When you are leading the presentation, do help draw out quieter candidates by creating a space for them to speak. Ensure that everyone has a say.

Commit to memory the following summary points to a successful group exercise:

- When it is your turn, introduce yourself by name.

- Tell your group what subject you are going to introduce.

- Explain that you are going to make a few brief points on the subject and then open it for discussion.

- Make your few brief points; be sure to speak clearly and with confidence.

● Invite other members of the group to contribute.

● If any member of the group has not had the chance to speak, then respectfully invite them to make a contribution.

● If someone makes a point with which you agree, then when they have finished speaking tell them so.

● When you speak to someone, remember to make eye contact with them.

Things you can do before the day

There is a lot you can do before the day to prepare for a group exercise. Here are a few suggestions that other candidates have used to good effect.

Plan something to say on core issues relevant to most subjects

You do not know the subject of your discussion in advance, although of course you know it will be related to the Fire Service. There are some issues that are relevant to almost every subject – these are called cross-cutting themes or core issues – and if you prepare something to say on these then you may be able to use this at an appropriate point in the discussions. By preparing in this way, you will not have to do all the thinking during the exercise, when you may well be feeling nervous and will be busy listening. Examples of cross-cutting themes that you might wish to research and prepare brief points on include:

● environmental issues relevant to the work of the Fire Service;

● health and safety;

● practical ways to implement the service's policy of equality of opportunity;

● inclusiveness for people with disabilities;

● the importance of serving diverse communities and all sections of society;

- the wide range of threats to public safety, including the threat from terrorism;

- the importance of planning for emergencies;

- giving priority to preventing fires;

- the Fire Service's desire to reach out more to the communities that it serves.

How to structure your introductory comments

We have seen that you may use the SWOT and PEST assessment tools in your preparation time just before your group exercise. You can also decide how you might broadly structure the introduction of your subject in advance:

1 Resolve to start by introducing yourself to the group.

2 Very briefly summarize the aims of the exercise.

3 Read out the subject to be discussed.

4 Again briefly, describe what you intend to go on to say.

5 Make your introductory points on the subject.

6 Open the subject up for discussion.

Broadly plan how you will introduce your subject

Introduce your subject and start the discussion by making just three or four separate points. Be sure that some are supportive while others highlight weaknesses. Always offer a solution to any weaknesses that you identify because then you will be judged as constructive. Plan to keep a point or two in reserve to introduce later if needed.

Don't worry if you do not get the opportunity to say everything you want. You must not dominate the discussion but show that you can contribute to it and help the group to develop the topic. Remember to provide space so that every member of the team has a chance to have a say. Do not forget that it is essential that you show enthusiasm throughout.

Get your timing right

You will not have long to introduce your subject before you open it up for discussion, so it is worth practising the timing. Try the following two exercises.

Exercise 1

- Decide how you are going to introduce yourself and practise what you have decided. Say aloud: 'Good morning everyone, my name is...'

- Decide on a statement that briefly summarizes the aim of the group exercise and practise saying this aloud.

- Decide how you might say that you now wish to open the subject up for discussion, and again practise saying it.

- Finally combine all three of the above and say them aloud one after the other.

Exercise 2

To get the introduction of your subject right, you need to have some experience of how long it will take to present a series of points with impact. Try to say too much or too little and you may end up disappointed with your performance.

Listen to a few public speakers, on the radio for example, and study how they make a point and how long it takes them.

Practise preparing a note of three or four separate points that will serve to introduce a subject – any subject (music, a film, yourself, your sport or exercise programme, anything that you know something about) – and then make these points aloud. Do not write out every word you wish to say but make only a few key-word notes and then introduce each point in your own words. Tape yourself and play it back in order to decide how you might improve what you have said. Prepare and practise making a series of these introductions – the subject is unimportant. To begin with you may feel uncomfortable doing this, but it will greatly help organize your thoughts and improve the way you will introduce your subject in the real exercise. It will also help you deal with any nervousness you may feel when doing it for real.

The interview

Do not even be one second late, and dress in a smart business-like manner. Firefighters are members of a uniformed service and you need to look and act the part.

You are very likely to be interviewed by more than one person and they may take it in turns to ask you questions. Try not to allow nerves to get the better of you. They are not trying to find fault or catch you out – they just want to identify your true potential. A serving firefighter may be present but this is not guaranteed. Instead the interview may be conducted by professionals in personnel with no direct experience of firefighting.

The interview will be highly structured. By this I mean that every candidate is likely to be given the same information and will be asked the same questions (but not necessarily the same follow-up questions). At times this may mean that the interview appears stilted.

An interview is an oral exam – you are judged on what you say in response to the questions asked of you. Everyone can improve on their interview performance, even someone who already interviews very well. If you are a quiet and reserved person, or not really used to talking about yourself and how you feel about things, then you will benefit most from practice and should begin straight away.

Obviously it is important to try your very best to pass at interview. To fail when you have succeeded in getting so far along the recruitment process is a great pity and a considerable disappointment. To start again and re-apply at the next call for applicants will mean that you have to pass the application form sift, written tests and physical fitness tests again before you have the opportunity to try once more at interview.

You will get better at interviews simply through the experience of being interviewed and by preparing for each interview. If you do fail, then ask the authority to tell you where you went wrong. Go over your interview and try to work out how you could do better. Straight after the interview it is worthwhile making a note of as many of the questions as you can remember. Keep researching the role of firefighter and the community in which you live. Make sure that you appreciate the importance of the service's equal opportunities policy and understand how it can be applied in practical day-to-day terms. Ensure that you understand the value that the service places on a diverse workforce and on serving all sections of the community. Practise answering the questions you were asked. Make sure that your answers demonstrate your understanding of these important issues.

Below you will find some practice interview questions, but first consider the description of the best method of preparing for an interview. Start your preparation by writing notes on what you want to say if it helps, but remember that you are not allowed to hand in an essay. Memorize your notes, then put them away and get practising at speaking.

You will not be allowed to make a speech that you have prepared. An interview is a conversation. That conversation could go in a number of directions and you must listen and respond to what the interviewer says. You must refer to all your positive experiences and each of your many qualities in answer to a relevant question asked of you. You must learn to adjust your answer in response to the question and make sure that your answer is to the point. You may then be asked follow-up questions based on what you have said, and you will have to provide a clear, relevant answer to them.

It can be a difficult balance. Try the method described below, and do also read one of the many interview books such as *Great Answers to Tough Interview Questions* by Martin Yates, published by Kogan Page.

A proven method for interview practice

To get good at interviews you have to practise in the correct way. Try the following method:

1 Revise what you wrote on your application form – you may be asked a question that relates to it.

2 Start with the information sent with your invitation to attend. It should include an outline of the day and what to expect at interview. The letter may suggest the broad subject areas that will be covered during the interview. If your letter did not

indicate the subject areas to be covered in the interview, then try these:

- why you want to be a firefighter;
- when you have shown commitment, determination and reliability;
- when you have worked as part of a team to overcome a difficult, stressful or unpleasant situation;
- what you understand by equality and community.

3 If you have not already done so, undertake some research. For example:

- Visit your local fire station and ask them if they are willing to show you around the station. Collect a copy of any leaflets on fire safety that are on display and read them.

- Research on the web the responsibilities and priorities of the Fire Service. Find out about the service's commitment to equality of opportunity both amongst its staff and in the provision of services to the general public. Think about how such a commitment can be delivered on a day-to-day basis by firefighters.

- Read about the service's efforts to improve the public's knowledge of fire prevention as well as firefighting. Work out how you think fire prevention could be improved.

- Visit your local library to find out more about the community in which you live and the services offered to the young and old and the socially excluded.

- Research the ethnic minority groups that live in your community, the minority religions and languages spoken.

- Learn what the responsibilities of firefighters are, the skills they must have and the knowledge they must acquire.

4 Take the subject areas from Point 2 and what you have established from the research described at Point 3, and work out what you could say at interview on each subject. Keep reviewing these responses until you are really familiar with them.

5 Now get someone to ask you some of the typical interview questions suggested below and, without looking at any notes, try to answer them. If you have done your research you should be able to provide clear, relevant answers to the questions. If you find it hard to give an answer other than one that is either very brief or very long, then you need to go back and review what you want to say until you understand it and can talk about it.

6 Once you start answering these questions with confidence, get your helper to ask the same question in a different way (I have suggested a few alternative ways of asking the same question below). Also, get them to start asking follow-up questions so that you have to think on your feet and adjust your answers.

7 Keep practising under these sorts of realistic interview situations until, despite feeling nervous on the day, you can talk confidently and clearly about yourself, the responsibilities of a firefighter, your community and equal opportunities.

Try making a video recording of yourself and playing it back to see for yourself how well you are doing.

Typical interview questions and follow-up questions

I have outlined 20 initial questions and many more possible follow-up questions that might be used to select firefighters at interview. Use them as part of the proven method of interview practice described above, and be sure to attend the interview with clear, well-structured answers to them all. The real interview will not comprise so many questions, but they will be just as difficult. This is one of many possible combinations of questions that you may be asked. Also, the follow-up questions may not be as they are described here. There are many, many possible alternatives and I have not covered them all.

1. Why do you want to be a firefighter?

Other ways that this question may be asked:

What experience can you bring to the role of a firefighter?

What have you done that qualifies you to be a firefighter?

Which of your qualities make you most suitable for the role of firefighter?

2. Tell us about an occasion when you have seen a difficult job through to its successful end.

Possible follow-up questions:

Can you tell us about another example?

How might you have done things better?

3. Describe a situation when you have motivated others to achieve something challenging.

Possible follow-up questions:

How did you feel about the outcome of this?

Can you think of another example?

How might you have done things differently if one of the people involved had been disabled?

How might you have done things differently if one of the people involved did not speak English?

4. Can you tell us of an occasion when you have shown a commitment to maintaining your knowledge and fitness?

Possible follow-up questions:

Can you tell us of something you are doing now to maintain your knowledge and fitness?

What more do you think you could be doing?

5. When have you worked with others to resolve a problem?
Possible follow-up question:
How did you inform your supervisor of this situation?

6. What do you think is one of the most important parts of a firefighter's work?
Possible follow-up question:
Can you describe another equally important role of firefighters?

7. Why do you think equality of opportunity is important in the Fire Service?
Possible follow-up questions:
Can you think of any other reason why equality of opportunities is important?
What does equal opportunities mean to you?
In practical terms how can the Fire Service apply its equal opportunities policy?

8. What more do you think the Fire Service could do in order to attract more women to apply for the post of firefighter?

9. Tell us of an occasion when you have had to deal with a stressful situation and how you coped with it.
Possible follow-up question:
How could you have done things better?

10. Tell us about an occasion when you have completed a task following written procedures.

Possible follow-up question:

Can you describe another occasion?

---

11. Tell me about something you have done that demonstrates commitment.

---

12. Can you describe an occasion when you have helped someone in your local community?

Possible follow-up questions:

How might you have dealt with things differently if the person you helped was a young person?

How might you have dealt with things differently if the person you helped was disabled?

---

13. We live in a multicultural society. Do you think this brings any advantages and if so what are they?

Possible follow-up questions:

Can you think of any other advantages?

Can you think of any disadvantages?

---

14. How do you think you might have improved your performance in the group exercise?

15. Describe to us a situation where you had to explain something to a group of people.

Possible follow-up questions:

How would you have dealt with this situation if one of the group could not speak English?

How would you have dealt with this situation if one of the group had impaired hearing?

---

16. Can you describe an occasion when you have shown empathy?

Possible follow-up question:

How do you think you could have shown greater empathy?

---

17. Tell us about a situation where you have had to deal with someone distressed or upset, and tell us how you managed the situation.

Possible follow-up questions:

Can you describe another occasion when you managed a situation where someone was distressed?

What else might you have done?

---

18. Describe to us how one of your hobbies or interests has served to prepare you for the role of firefighter.

Possible follow-up question:

How have any other of your hobbies or interests helped prepare you for the role?

19. Why do you think community relations are important to the Fire Service?
Possible follow-up question:
> What more do you think the Fire Service could do to ensure that it enjoys the trust of the people within your community?

20. Describe a situation where you have had to change the way you did something.
Possible follow-up question:
> Tell us how you feel in general about change.

Physical tests

At one or possibly two points in the recruitment process you will face a series of fitness tests. They are likely to involve tests of both your aerobic fitness and strength. All of the tests involve tasks relevant to the work of a firefighter; many will be undertaken in full protective clothing and involve equipment used daily by firefighters (these are called work sample tests).

It is important to understand that, while there will be minimum standards that you must achieve in order to pass, and these standards are high, these tests are not so difficult that only the super-fit or super-strong can pass them. The majority of men and women can pass these tests or learn to pass them. The key to success is confidence, technique and the achievement and maintenance of a high level of overall fitness.

The previous national standards and the new standards involve any of the following physical tests:

Examples of aerobic fitness and strength tests:

- running (the bleb test);
- lung capacity;

- hand pull;
- back pull.

Examples of work-sampled physical tests (often completed in full firefighting gear and in some cases while wearing breathing apparatus):

- extending a ladder;
- climbing ladders;
- deploying a hose;
- moving through a confined space with restricted visibility;
- carrying firefighter equipment.

In the case of any of these tests an administrator will explain the task to you, and in most, if not all, instances will demonstrate what you have to do. Information will also be provided in the invitation to attend for the tests. This information will include details of what to bring in terms of suitable clothing and footwear. Appropriate facilities will be made available for you to change and shower.

No matter how fit you are, begin a programme of exercise that is similar to the tasks on which you will be tested. You should include exercises to improve your aerobic fitness, upper body strength and running. Train throughout the period of your application as it will serve you well both in meeting the physical challenge of the application stage and during your initial firefighter fitness training.

Consider getting professional advice

Fitness advisers are available at sports clubs and gyms and will help you to devise a personal training programme to suit your circumstances. They are also able to make assessments of your current fitness and progress in becoming fitter. Explain that you are facing the firefighter fitness test and take along a description of the physical test that has been sent to you.

If it is some time since you have undertaken strenuous physical exercise, then start your programme of training straight away. The fact that you are not as fit as you used to be will in no way exclude you from becoming a firefighter. All you must do is put the situation right and get down to some serious weeks or months of determined and frequent training. Consider making an appointment with your GP before you start in earnest, explain what you intend to do and ask if there is any reason why you should not begin such a programme.

If you sustain an injury or are unwell just before your test and fear this may adversely affect your performance, then contact the fire authority and explain the problem. They may agree to you attending at a later date but are likely to require a doctor's note confirming that the reason is genuine.

Medicals

Towards the end of the application process, if you have passed all the stages up to that point, you will be asked to undertake a medical examination. As previously mentioned, certain medical conditions may be considered incompatible with the role of firefighter. However, each case is different, so a decision on the individual's ability to do the job should be made by the medical practitioner. It is understandably a great disappointment for any candidate to overcome so many hurdles in the recruitment process and then fail at almost the final stage.

If you know of any reason or have any condition that may mean that you might fail the medical, it is probably best to make enquiries before you progress down the recruitment process only to be rejected on health grounds.

Ask the authority's recruitment team whether or not your condition could be an issue. Your GP may be able to provide some indication of whether or not your health may exclude you from the service but note that while this may be a useful indicator, only the fire authority doctor can say for certain. By asking in advance, at least you will be forewarned of a potential problem.

Some candidates arrange for a private eyesight test. Once they have a positive result they can then be sure that they can progress with their application in the knowledge that their eyesight will not let them down at the medical.

References

With your prior consent, a number of references will be taken and checks made. This will occur at various stages of the application process and may include:

- references from your employment or study going back some years;

- a check to confirm you have a right to work in the UK;

- a police record check to confirm that you have declared any criminal convictions;

- references confirming any community or voluntary work.

Be sure that you detail accurately the names and addresses, including the postcodes, of all referees. Omissions or errors can lead to significant delays and can prevent you from starting employment with the service until satisfactory replies have been obtained. It is well worth writing to or calling your referees, asking permission to use them and explaining who might contact them. Take this opportunity to stress how important it is that they kindly reply as soon as is convenient.

Many applicants fear that they do not have anyone suitable as a referee. This is perhaps because they have moved between jobs or not had paid work for some time or have been self-employed. If one of these situations applies to you then you will need to do a bit more work than someone who has been in the same job since school or college, but otherwise there is no reason why you should not be able to provide acceptable references.

Consider approaching the fire authority recruitment team for guidance. Briefly describe your situation and ask, given your circumstances, who they recommend would be best to approach for a reference.

Take care to disclose any periods of unemployment or long holidays, and if you are unemployed give serious thought to undertaking some unpaid community or voluntary work. It will mean that you update your skills and should provide you with a reference.

If you are self-employed or a subcontractor then it may be acceptable for you to provide a number of your recent customers as referees.

If you have moved between lots of jobs then start straight away, contacting each employer, seeking permission to use them as a referee and obtaining their full postal address. Explain what you are hoping to do, how important it is to you and that you are sorry to have to trouble them. They may be willing to confirm dates of employment and any other relevant details of which you are unsure.

CHAPTER 6

Answers and explanations

Chapter 2, The application forms

1   *Explanation*: as I have previously explained, there is no situation where a firefighter would be anything other than honest.

2   *Explanation*: the effects of some recreational drugs are long-lasting and they may well affect your ability to do your job many, many hours later. For this reason, using such drugs even in the privacy of your own home may not be a personal matter and is likely to be something the Fire Service would be very concerned about. See your response to q56 to check that you are being consistent in your responses.

3   *Explanation*: the Fire Service might well expect you to disagree with this statement. After all someone shouting and screaming might need help! Even if that person is not in need of help, the service would expect a firefighter to provide the same level of care and attention irrespective of who people are or how they conduct themselves. Compare your answer to this question with your responses to q40 and 78 to check that you are being consistent in your answers.

4 *Explanation*: as a firefighter you should be comfortable discussing something when you hold a different opinion from others. You should not feel that it is necessary to change the subject. Check your answers to q29 and 42 for consistency.

5 *Explanation*: to be opinionated is to be full of your own views and not to consider the views of others enough. In a firefighter such an approach would always be a bad thing.

6 *Explanation*: some people use knowledge in order to exercise power, hence the saying 'knowledge is power'. A firefighter should use knowledge to serve the community not to exercise power and so would agree that knowledge is not power.

7 *Explanation*: firefighters sometimes have to make difficult decisions and no doubt they find these decisions difficult, but not impossible.

8 *Explanation*: firefighters might in the course of their careers have to do something that goes against their personal beliefs. For example, some religious believers do not think it right to work on a Sunday, but the work of a firefighter is 24/7 and it is not practical for firefighters to be excused from working Sundays.

9 *Explanation*: communication is an important part of a firefighter's role and previous experience of explaining things to groups of people would help support your application.

10 *Explanation*: when on duty firefighters live in close proximity to each other and they need to get on. For this reason compromises are often made and they are right in terms of ensuring a good working relationship among colleagues.

11 *Explanation*: the fire station can most definitely be a part of the local community like any other public building. Check that your answer is consistent with your responses to q26 and 91.

12 *Explanation*: firefighters have to be straight-speaking with each other. This does not mean they say whatever they think, but they must be able to explain something they might find difficult rather than bottling it up by keeping it to themselves. For this reason you would not agree with this statement. Check that your answer to q23 is consistent with this answer.

13 *Explanation*: if you can speak a second language well, then be sure to agree with this statement, and make sure that you refer to this useful skill in one of your responses elsewhere on your application form and at interview.

14 *Explanation*: you cannot know if you would like people until you have met them so it would be wrong to say that there are nearly always a few people whom you do not like. You should therefore agree with this statement.

15 *Explanation*: to agree with this statement would count against your application to be a firefighter. Yes firefighters are active, but they can concentrate and they can be patient.

16 *Explanation*: it is true that everyone will make mistakes and employers do prefer that they are disclosed at the first opportunity and that we work to correct them. Compare your answer with your response to q31 to see that you are being consistent.

17 *Explanation*: if you believe that actions speak louder than words then it suggests that your word is not as reliable as your actions, and this is not something that would support your application to be a firefighter. Check your answer with the answers you have given to q20 and 43.

18 *Explanation*: teamwork is as important as the communication of fire safety but it is no more important so you should be able to agree with this statement.

19 *Explanation*: firefighters have to take risks but they are calculated risks and far more likely to be kept to an absolute minimum when approached thoughtfully and carefully. Check your answer for consistency with q32, 47 and 65.

20 *Explanation*: when carrying out their duties firefighters would never be expected to lie and even the occasional lie would be unacceptable. Compare your answer with those to q17 and 43 to check that you are being consistent.

21 *Explanation*: firefighters do follow procedures relating to much of their work, and candidates who indicate that they work well following procedures will be seen as suitable for the role. Compare your answer to this question with your responses to q24, 41 and 57.

22   *Explanation*: every employer would hope that their employees agreed with this statement and helped them stop inappropriate behaviour at work. Check your responses to q68, 92 and 96 for consistency.

23   *Explanation*: if you say you find something very difficult then you are admitting that it is something you will find hard to do. Discussing how they feel is an important way in which firefighters cope with the stressful and distressing situations they sometimes face. Most people find it difficult to explain their personal feelings; if you find it very difficult then, in preparation for a career as a firefighter, you may need to learn how to express your personal feelings more readily. Check your answer to q12 to ensure that your responses are consistent.

24   *Explanation*: I'm sure you agree that it is advisable to follow the advice in a safety notice. So you should have agreed with the statement 'it is not advisable not to follow the advice in a safety notice'. If this is unclear then leave out the first NOT in the sentence and then respond to the statement 'it is... advisable not to follow the advice in a safety notice'. It should be clear that the answer to this is to disagree. Now put the first NOT back and it changes your disagreement to agreement. Be sure that your answer is consistent with your responses to q21, 41 and 57.

25   *Explanation*: a firefighter works hard to try to ensure that everyone in society, including those who can't speak English, receives the same help and assistance as anyone else. For this reason a firefighter might well disagree with this statement.

26   *Explanation*: firefighters do constantly train but they also find the time for the important job of promoting fire safety and maintaining good relations with members of the general public. One of the ways they do this is to open up the fire station and invite people to look around. Compare your answer with your responses to q11 and 91 to check that you are being consistent.

27   *Explanation*: the presence of a woman in a team, attractive or otherwise, should have no bearing on how the men present act. If the men try to impress a woman member of the team it might well amount to inappropriate behaviour and result in disciplinary action. Check your answer is consistent with your responses to q45 and 60.

28   *Explanation*: agreeing with this statement strongly suggests that the work of a firefighter is not for you.

29   *Explanation*: to be dogmatic is to assert your opinions as the only true ones, and this is not a quality that would make for a team player. See your responses to q4 and 42 for consistency.

30   *Explanation*: firefighters are not their own bosses, so to agree with this statement would involve presenting yourself as someone who is not very well suited for the role.

31   *Explanation*: most employers would prefer to hear about something that has gone wrong as soon as possible and would not welcome a situation where a mistake is not reported until it has been resolved. This is because the attempt to correct the situation may not succeed or may even make matters worse, and then what might have been a relatively minor issue may become something much more serious. Check your answer here to see if it is consistent with your answer to q16.

32   *Explanation*: firefighters follow orders but they also raise any concerns they may have in order that the decision that gives rise to the order is the best one. Check your answer for consistency with q19, 47 and 65.

33   *Explanation*: you should disagree with this statement unless you want to give the impression that you have some preconceptions and prejudices about whom you like and dislike. Check your answer to q14 to see that you have responded consistently.

34   *Explanation*: you should be able to agree with this statement as a commitment to staying fit is an important part of a firefighter's job, though it is not more or less important than being able to show the courage to see a difficult job done (in other words to be brave).

35 *Explanation*: firefighters work shifts and this involves being on duty at times when their friends and family are out enjoying themselves. This is an unavoidable part of the job of a firefighter and is something that you must be prepared to do.

36 *Explanation*: firefighters routinely take orders from more senior colleagues and anyone in the role would need to be happy to take orders. Check your answer to q44 to see that you are being consistent in your responses.

37 *Explanation*: to agree with this statement would suggest that you are very shy and would find it hard to form working relationships with colleagues or people from your local community. Such relationships are essential to the work of a firefighter and you should therefore work to overcome any shyness so that you are able to disagree with this statement.

38 *Explanation*: derisive means nasty, and at work it would be wrong, not clever, to make such remarks.

39 *Explanation*: firefighters have a clearly defined role and set of responsibilities; for this reason you would expect someone well suited for the role to agree with this statement.

40 *Explanation*: the Fire Service expects firefighters to treat everyone equally, irrespective of what they think of them. Check your answers to q3 and 78 to see if you are being consistent in your responses.

41 *Explanation*: the role of a firefighter necessarily has procedures that for safety reasons must be followed, and these procedures are best written down. For this reason you should be comfortable about agreeing with the statement. Check that you have been consistent with this answer and your responses to q21, 24 and 57.

42 *Explanation*: in life more that one view can be right and it is not necessarily the case that if one view is right all others are wrong. Such a view might suggest someone who is dogmatic in their opinions. Check your responses to q4 and 29 for consistency.

43 *Explanation*: keeping your word is a great quality and one that any fire authority would want the firefighters to adhere to. See your responses to q17 and 20 to check that you are being consistent in your approach.

44   *Explanation*: agreement with this statement means that you are comfortable with being given orders, as most firefighters are. Check your answer to q36 for consistency.

45   *Explanation*: our work should be organized in a way that ensures both men and women are equally able to complete the tasks. For this reason you should feel able to disagree with this statement. Check that your answer is consistent with your responses to q27 and 60.

46   *Explanation*: you should be comfortable to disagree with this statement. It should be obvious to everyone that bad language is inappropriate at work and is something we should refrain from.

47   *Explanation*: firefighters work as a team and support each other in the face of adversity. They value each other's safety as highly as their own. Check your answer for consistency with q19, 32 and 65.

48   *Explanation*: telling people that you agree with what they have said is an affirming, positive thing and encouraging and constructive. Contributing to a conversation in such a way is the sort of thing the assessors look for during the group exercise.

49   *Explanation*: this is really a question of honesty, which is something always expected of a firefighter. Check your answer to q72 to confirm that you are being consistent in your responses.

50   *Explanation*: the work of a firefighter is physical, and an emergency may well involve you having to labour manually in hot, dirty conditions.

51   *Explanation*: firefighters receive orders but in an emergency they also give them, for example to direct the general public away from danger. Someone who lacked the confidence to give orders might need to develop the necessary confidence before taking up the role of firefighter.

52   *Explanation*: people from some cultural backgrounds and some shy people may be reluctant to look you directly in the eye or shake your hand, and this is something that should not greatly concern us.

53 *Explanation*: to agree with this statement would not support your application to be a firefighter. Someone who gets bored easily is probably someone who lacks motivation. Firefighters unavoidably spend time ready to respond to an emergency, and someone who hated waiting for something to happen would not enjoy this aspect of the job.

54 *Explanation*: a fire authority would want its applicant firefighters to agree with this statement. The job requires a commitment to continually develop your knowledge and skills and to maintain your fitness throughout your career. These are not light commitments and would not suit someone seeking an easy life.

55 *Explanation*: it is never appropriate to make a racist remark.

56 *Explanation*: you should be happy to agree with this statement. If drinking in your spare time affects your ability to do your job safely then it is your employer's business. Firefighters work shifts and for this reason they must take great care that they do not compromise their ability to do their job by, for example, drinking before a shift. Review your answer to q2 to check that you are being consistent in your responses.

57 *Explanation*: to agree with this statement would suggest that you may not consider it important to familiarize yourself with the safe operation of equipment before you use it, and this might be judged to be an unsafe approach. Check your answer is consistent with your responses to q21, 24 and 41.

58 *Explanation*: both these aspects of a firefighter's role are essential to the job and it is not possible to say that one is more important than the other.

59 *Explanation*: if you can't agree with this statement it does not mean that you will not pass through to the next stage of the firefighter recruitment process. The service extensively trains firefighters in the use of all their equipment and is looking for people who have the potential to do the job rather than already having the skills and experience.

60 *Explanation*: women can make exemplary firefighters and if you succeed in your ambition to become one you will meet some. But take care when answering questions that involve a double negative. You should have agreed with this statement because it says it is NOT true that women do not make good firefighters. Check that your answer is consistent with your responses to q27 and 45.

61 *Explanation*: teamwork is very important in the role of firefighter and so the candidate best suited for the role is someone who would agree with this statement. See your responses to q73 and 97 for consistency.

62 *Explanation*: you should have no difficulty agreeing with this statement.

63 *Explanation*: aggression is never appropriate behaviour at work and there are no circumstances when it would be something you should be willing to demonstrate as a firefighter. Check your answer to q66 to see if you are being consistent in your responses to these questions.

64 *Explanation*: being able to listen and, equally important, demonstrating that you can listen is a skill that will support your application to be a firefighter. When you attend the assessment day you must take part in a group exercise that seeks to assess, among a number of things, your ability to listen and how well you can incorporate what you have heard into your own views.

65 *Explanation*: you might disagree with this in the context of making money in business or in sport, but in the role of a firefighter success is not dependent on boldness but on training, teamwork and working with the community. Check your answers to q19, 32 and 47 for consistency.

66 *Explanation*: no employer would want employees to raise their voices during a discussion or conversation. So you should agree that it would be wrong to do so. Check your answer to q63 to see that you are being consistent in your responses to these questions.

67 *Explanation*: many employers would expect you to agree with this statement. Strong language, even if only moderately strong, is not appropriate at work and is easily avoided. Some colleagues will find moderately strong language objectionable and their sensitivities should be respected. See your response to q80 to check that you are being consistent in the way you answer related questions.

68 *Explanation*: every responsible employer would expect their staff to disagree with this statement. Bullying is not a private matter but something that is unacceptable in the workplace. Check your answers to q22, 92 and 96 for consistency.

69 *Explanation*: to be sarcastic means to mock someone, and in work it is not clever but inappropriate if you are sarcastic.

70 *Explanation*: a firefighter will obviously be required sometimes to work up ladders and at heights. Previous experience in this would be useful but it is not essential for you to succeed in your application.

71 *Explanation*: to agree with this statement would suggest a confidence in dealing in social situations that would serve you well in the role of firefighter.

72 *Explanation*: you should agree with this statement; every employer would prefer to hear bad news early so that they can help put right the problem rather than find out about it later when perhaps things have become much more complicated. Check your answer to q49 to see that you are being consistent in your responses.

73 *Explanation*: it is true that a problem shared is a problem halved and this is the great benefit of working as a team. Check your answers to q61 and 97 for consistency.

74 *Explanation*: firefighters spend time on call ready to respond to an emergency; for this reason to admit that you get restless when waiting would not be something that supported your application.

75 *Explanation*: this is a slightly unfair question as so few people can honestly say they have never lied. If you come across such a question then be truthful. Admitting that you have in your life lied is a response that on its own should not mean that your application is rejected.

76   *Explanation*: firefighters are expected to be active in their local community and to be able to communicate with people drawn from all sections of that community. People who take the trouble to know their neighbours may well possess important qualities that make for good firefighters.

77   *Explanation*: most contracts of employment require you to report to your employer a fact such as the dishonesty of a colleague, and most employers would wish you to agree with this statement.

78   *Explanation*: the Fire Service expects you to treat colleagues and the general public with the same professionalism and courtesy, irrespective of your personal feeling towards them. Check your answers to q3 and 40 to see that they are consistent with your answer to this question.

79   *Explanation*: firefighters maintain their fitness and continually develop their skills and knowledge throughout their career; such a commitment would not be something that someone who agreed with this statement would find easy to fulfil.

80   *Explanation*: most employers would expect you to disagree with this statement. In every workplace jokes are told but it is implied in the statement that someone does not find them funny and when this happens the joking should stop. Compare your answer to your response to q67 to check that your responses are consistent.

81   *Explanation*: to agree with this statement would support your application; firefighters are active people and they keep active by maintaining their physical fitness.

82   *Explanation*: it is not true that being strong is more important than showing commitment to the role of a firefighter. Firefighters carry out difficult tasks but they rely on technique, their training and teamwork as much as their strength to achieve these tasks.

83   *Explanation*: a firefighter would agree with this statement because charity is about helping others in need, and a firefighter will help people in need irrespective of who they are. Check q98 for the consistency of your answers.

84 *Explanation*: this is something you should be happy to agree with. Work is not somewhere where we should show our temper or have to be subjected to colleagues losing their tempers.

85 *Explanation*: taking anything from work without permission is stealing, and the fact that lots of people do something does not make it right.

86 *Explanation*: you should be happy to agree with this statement and should ensure that at interview and during the group exercise all your contributions and answers can be interpreted constructively.

87 *Explanation*: no employer would want employees who admitted to finding it difficult to control themselves. At work we act professionally and according to our terms and conditions of employment. To lose control would be unacceptable, especially in a critical role such as a firefighter's.

88 *Explanation*: a firefighter must both deal sympathetically with people who are distressed and demonstrate a commitment to equal opportunities. Neither of these essential attributes is more important than the other. They are both equally important to the role.

89 *Explanation*: at work it is not appropriate to lose your temper even if it is only briefly. You should disagree with this statement because if something is upsetting you to the point where you are finding it difficult to cope then you should discuss it with someone and try to resolve it that way.

90 *Explanation*: you should be happy to agree with this statement, and when you attend the assessment centre you should encourage and support the other candidates even though you are in competition with them for the job!

91 *Explanation*: you can strongly agree with this statement. Local knowledge includes, for example, knowing the shortest route to the location of an emergency or knowing that a street might be temporarily closed for roadworks. It also involves knowing community elders, representatives and leaders. Compare your answer with your responses to q11 and 26 to check that you are being consistent.

92 *Explanation*: no employer would welcome such action nor would they want an employee to consider this a suitable response at work. Bullying is a serious issue and the appropriate response is to report it and help the employer to prevent its reoccurrence. Check your answers to q22, 68 and 96 for consistency.

93 *Explanation*: we all have to work to earn money but this is not the primary reason why people want to become firefighters. You can earn as much or more money in many, many jobs but there are few other jobs that you will find so rewarding in terms of serving your community.

94 *Explanation*: I would expect the Fire Service to prefer the candidate who disagrees with this statement. Firefighting is the glamorous side of the profession; it is obviously very important and what you will spend a great deal of time training for, but not more important than work to prevent fires.

95 *Explanation*: if you disagree with this statement then you are admitting that you might act inappropriately at work rather than explaining to a colleague or superior that you are finding something difficult.

96 *Explanation*: every responsible employer would want you to agree with this statement as they may not always know that a problem has arisen and once informed can take action to resolve it. Check your answers to q22, 68 and 92 for consistency.

97 *Explanation*: the more adverse the conditions the more important it is that firefighters work as a team. For this reason you should not agree with this statement. Check your responses to q61 and 73 for consistency.

98 *Explanation*: the Fire Service is committed to providing the same high standard of assistance to everyone irrespective of who they are or whether we know them.

99 *Explanation*: some people are very house-proud and may ask you to take off your shoes before you come in; in some cultures it is normal to take off your shoes before entering any home. So this is definitely a statement you should agree with as such a request is not something you should say you would find annoying.

100 *Explanation*: you should be able to state a number of good reasons why we no longer use the term 'fireman'. The Fire Service long ago stopped using the term because it wants to encourage more women to become firefighters. You should avoid using the term, and be sure not to use it when you attend for interview.

Chapter 3, Written tests and practice questions

Understanding information

The first 50 practice questions

Passage 1

Q1   *Answer*: False.
Explanation: the passage reports that the trainee was wearing a firefighter's protective suit, boots and helmet.

Q2   *Answer*: Cannot say.
Explanation: the passage states that the fire was in a room, which could be on board a ship or on land.

Q3   *Answer*: True.

Q4   *Answer*: True.

Q5   *Answer*: False.
Explanation: the passage says that the centre was in Gosport.

Q6   *Answer*: Cannot say.
Explanation: the passage states that poorly maintained electrical equipment and deposits of oil and grease are most likely to cause a fire on a ship. You cannot tell from the given information whether it is electrical equipment or oil and grease that causes the most fires.

Q7   *Answer*: True.

Q8   *Answer*: Cannot say.
     Explanation: the passage does not provide any advice on
     this subject.

Q9   *Answer*: True.

Q10 *Answer*: Cannot say.
     Explanation: whilst most people may agree with this
     statement, the passage does not comment on this issue
     so you cannot answer it from the information provided.

Passage 2

Q11 *Answer*: False.
     Explanation: the passage states that there are often many
     aerosol cans on boats.

Q12 *Answer*: False.
     Explanation: the trainees had first-hand experience of foam,
     dry powder and carbon dioxide extinguishers.

Q13 *Answer*: True.

Q14 *Answer*: False.

Q15 *Answer*: True.

Q16 *Answer*: False.
     Explanation: the passage contains no reference to the
     effects of smoke.

Q17 *Answer*: Cannot say.
     Explanation: the previous passage commented on the
     content of the course but this information cannot be used in
     a different passage.

Q18 *Answer*: Cannot say.
     Explanation: the passage makes no comment on the
     applications of a foam-filled extinguisher.

Q19 *Answer*: True.
     Explanation: the passage states that the flame can travel
     at 5 metres per second; $7 \times 5 = 35$, which is further than
     25 metres.

Q20 *Answer*: Cannot say.
     Explanation: the passage does not comment on the
     qualities of foam extinguishers.

Passage 3

Q21 *Answer*: True.
Explanation: the passage states that this is one of the items that a fire emergency plan should cover.

Q22 *Answer*: True.

Q23 *Answer*: True.

Q24 *Answer*: False.
Explanation: the passage does not make any specific statement that a fire alarm must be fitted.

Q25 *Answer*: False.
Explanation: a fire emergency plan would cover the possibility of an electrical fault but this is not the point of the passage.

Passage 4

Q26 *Answer*: True.

Q27 *Answer*: False.
Explanation: the passage says that 'it is important to make sure that people do not use lifts' and you can reasonably assume that this includes people with a disability.

Q28 *Answer*: Cannot say.
Explanation: the passage does not comment on what people should do once evacuated.

Q29 *Answer*: False.
Explanation: the passage makes no reference to fire wardens so the statement is false.

Q30 *Answer*: True.
Explanation: it is clear from the passage that on discovery of a fire you should raise the alarm and assist in the evacuation of people before considering fighting the fire.

Passage 5

Q31 *Answer*: True.
Explanation: the passage states that when tackling a fire you should position yourself between the fire and the way out. When fighting the fire you will be facing it, so it is likely that your back will be facing your exit.

Q32   *Answer*: True.
   Explanation: class A fires are stated to be solid objects and
   a table is a solid object.

Q33   *Answer*: True.

Q34   *Answer*: False.
   Explanation: the passage only refers to places of work, not
   to homes.

Q35   *Answer*: False.
   Explanation: the passage describes which extinguisher to
   use on type A, B and C fires but does not state the
   advantages of the various types.

Passage 6

Q36   *Answer*: True.

Q37   *Answer*: False.
   Explanation: the passage states that smoke and fire can
   incapacitate people as the fire spreads. They need not be
   trapped for this danger to exist.

Q38   *Answer*: Cannot say.
   Explanation: this passage does not comment on the
   provision of firefighting equipment or training in its use.

Q39   *Answer*: Cannot say.
   Explanation: the passage makes no reference to smoke
   alarms.

Q40   *Answer*: True.

Passage 7

Q41   *Answer*: False.
   Explanation: the passage states that all three are needed for
   a fire to occur, not that if all three are present a fire will
   occur.

Q42   *Answer*: False.
   Explanation: the passage states that oxygen is also found in
   a chemical form.

Q43   *Answer*: True.

Q44 *Answer*: Cannot say.
        Explanation: the passage does not range the examples in
        terms of flammability.

Q45 *Answer*: True.

Passage 8

Q46 *Answer*: True.

Q47 *Answer*: True.
        Explanation: this is clearly stated in the last sentence of the
        passage.

Q48 *Answer*: False.
        Explanation: the passage makes no comment on this issue.

Q49 *Answer*: False.
        Explanation: it is stated in the passage that an assessment
        might also require an assessment of whether or not the
        risks are acceptable and whether anything can be done to
        reduce them.

Q50 *Answer*: True.

Another 50 understanding-information questions

Passage 1

Q1 *Answer*: False.
       Explanation: the passage does not comment on the issue of
       nuisance children.

Q2 *Answer*: True.
       Explanation: the passage states that you can take your
       complaint to a local mediation service.

Q3 *Answer*: True.
       Explanation: the passage states that the term lacks an
       agreed definition and this means there is not a commonly
       held definition.

Q4 *Answer*: True.
       Explanation: you could take a case of racial harassment to
       your housing office, but you could and probably should

take a complaint of racial harassment to the police as it is a very serious matter.

Q5   *Answer*: False.

Explanation: it is stated in the passage that the police only deal with severe antisocial behaviour; an untidy garden is described in the passage as an example of a minor transgression so the police would not get involved in such a case, irrespective of the residency of the complainant or perpetrator.

Passage 2

Q6   *Answer*: True.

Explanation: it is stated in the passage that people who do not do voluntary work do not enjoy living in their area as much as people who do. It is also stated that people who do not do voluntary work do not feel that people are inclined to help each other, while people who do voluntary work believe that people there are willing to help each other. It is reasonable to conclude from this that the former have less positive views of their community than people who do voluntary work.

Q7   *Answer*: False.

Explanation: the passage does not state this.

Q8   *Answer*: False.

Explanation: the passage does not state that they do not enjoy living in their area but that they enjoy living in their area less than people who do voluntary work.

Q9   *Answer*: Cannot say.

Explanation: the passage does not say whether or not people who do no voluntary work trust other people in their community, so it is not possible to say.

Q10   *Answer*: True.

Explanation: the passage states that almost everyone who does voluntary work has a positive opinion and almost everyone does not mean everyone. This means that a few people who do voluntary work do not have a positive view of their community, though the vast majority do.

Passage 3

Q11 *Answer*: True.
Explanation: the passage states that Credit Unions offer members loans at a low rate of interest.

Q12 *Answer*: Cannot say.
Explanation: the passage does not say how you can draw on savings so we cannot tell if this statement is true or false.

Q13 *Answer*: False.
Explanation: the passage states that members can open accounts, so not everyone: only members.

Q14 *Answer*: False.
Explanation: the passage states that the average Credit Union has 3,500 members so a union with 2,000 members would not be considered large.

Q15 *Answer*: Cannot say.
Explanation: while the passage states that Credit Unions pay high rates of interest to savers and charge low rates to borrowers, it does not compare their rates with those of high-street banks so we cannot say if the statement is true or false.

Passage 4

Q16 *Answer*: Cannot say.
Explanation: the passage states that a second reason for people getting involved is that they are new to an area, not that this is the second most common reason for getting involved in the community. It is possible that it is the second most common reason, but we do not know because the passage does not provide information on this point, so the correct answer is Cannot say.

Q17 *Answer*: False.
Explanation: of the three reasons given in the passage, one is when a tragedy occurs and this is a negative reason rather than a good reason for becoming involved in your community although good may come from it.

Q18 *Answer*: Cannot say.

Explanation: this may well be true but if we base our answer on the information given in the passage we are unable to say whether it is the case or not, so the correct answer is Cannot say.

Q19 *Answer*: False.

Explanation: raising money for a local charity might well be an example of community involvement but it is not one of the examples given in the passage.

Q20 *Answer*: True.

Explanation: the passage only considers the reasons people become involved in their local community and does not consider why people might get involved outside their local community, for example nationally or regionally.

Passage 5

Q21 *Answer*: False.

Explanation: the passage states that whole communities can also suffer social exclusion.

Q22 *Answer*: True.

Explanation: the passage states that it is common for people to suffer more than one of the causes and so the author is likely to agree that an individual who suffers one cause is likely to suffer others too.

Q23 *Answer*: Cannot say.

Explanation: the passage does not provide any information on whether or not social exclusion is found in wealthy societies, so if we stick to the information provided we cannot say whether this statement is true or false.

Q24 *Answer*: True.

Explanation: the passage states that a lack of key skills may cause social exclusion, and it is reasonable to infer that not being able to read or write is an example of lacking a key skill.

Q25 *Answer*: False.

Explanation: the passage does not comment on the possibility of solutions to social exclusion.

Passage 6

Q26 *Answer*: True.
Explanation: the passage states that 9 per cent of the population of Manchester identified themselves as Asian or Asian British, 6 per cent as Black or Black British, 3 per cent as mixed race and 2 per cent as Chinese or another ethnic group. This totals 20 per cent.

Q27 *Answer*: False.
Explanation: the passage states that many people from Manchester have Irish ancestry, not that they describe themselves as Irish.

Q28 *Answer*: Cannot say.
Explanation: the passage states that the Jewish community of Manchester is the second-largest Jewish community in the UK; it does not detail which religious community is the second-largest in the city and this information cannot be inferred from the passage, so the answer is Cannot say.

Q29 *Answer*: True.
Explanation: the passage opens with the statement that the population of Manchester has declined.

Q30 *Answer*: True.
Explanation: the passage describes large Muslim and Jewish religious communities and so it is fair to conclude that the city is religiously diverse.

Passage 7

Q31 *Answer*: A.
Explanation: the passage states that 90 per cent of Travellers no longer live in caravans, but this still leaves 10 per cent who do. It is correct to say that the vast majority no longer live in caravans.

Q32 *Answer*: C.
Explanation: it could be true that the term 'Gypsy' is derived from the word 'Egyptian' but this point is not made in the passage. In the context of the passage it is not possible to say whether A is true or false. The passage does describe

Gypsies as historically having a nomadic way of life. B is wrong because most of them no longer lead a fully nomadic way of life. The passage does not indicate whether the term Gypsy is rarely heard nowadays.

Q33 *Answer*: B.

Explanation: the passage describes the occupations of Travellers so you can infer that the author would not agree that Travellers do not work.

Q34 *Answer*: A.

Explanation: the passage states that the Gypsies' and Irish Travellers' nomadic way of life goes back far into antiquity and this means the same as in the very distant past.

Q35 *Answer*: C.

Explanation: the passage states that a sizeable minority fail to complete their education, therefore most do. No information is provided on how well or otherwise the children do in exams.

Passage 8

Q36 *Answer*: D.

Explanation: the passage is about providing translation and interpretation and other services to ensure good practice in the promotion and delivery of services. So D is the best summary offered of what the passage is about.

Q37 *Answer*: B.

Explanation: the passage states that interpreters meet people and translators work with written material, so answer B is the closest to what the passage says.

Q38 *Answer*: C.

Explanation: from reading the passage it can be concluded that the issue is not only about people's command of English or whether they have only been in the UK for a short time. The passage indicates that disabled people may also need the services of an interpreter. These people may have been in the UK all their lives and speak English as their mother tongue. They may still need an interpreter because of the language barrier.

Q39 *Answer*: B.

Explanation: the passage describes the contribution that can be made with audiotapes and induction loops, so it does allow technology to play a role in giving equal access to services.

Q40 *Answer*: A.

Explanation: the passage states that the number of languages spoken in the UK has recently increased. The passage does not comment on the timescale of this increase.

Passage 9

Q41 *Answer*: D.

Explanation: the passage does not comment on whether or not you can take up a grievance after you have left a job, nor does it say that everyone has the option of taking a grievance to an employment tribunal. It states that if you are unable to resolve a grievance informally you should write to your employer.

Q42 *Answer*: A.

Explanation: it is allowed for someone to accompany you to the meetings but this point is not covered in the passage, so we can rule out as wrong suggested answers B and C. You will only attend two meetings if you appeal after the first, which is stated in A, the correct answer.

Q43 *Answer*: A.

Explanation: this is a correct summary of the points made in the second paragraph of the passage. A meeting would not necessarily be your initial request nor would approaching an employment tribunal.

Q44 *Answer*: C.

Explanation: transparent means clear and in the context of the passage it means an easily understood set of procedures. Obscure is the opposite of transparent.

Q45 *Answer*: B.

Explanation: the passage states that you should first try to resolve a grievance informally, so without using the official grievance procedure. You might first talk to your employer about how you feel before you write to them notifying them of your grievance.

Passage 10

Q46   *Answer*: D.

Explanation: the passage reports that people who answer certain questions one way are more likely to believe that racial tension has decreased, not that it has in fact decreased or increased.

Q47   *Answer*: A.

Explanation: the passage states that people who say they have friends drawn from a mixture of racial groups also said that there was less racial prejudice now than there was five years ago. Someone who felt racial prejudice was less prevalent now than five years ago might also agree with statement A that they have friends of different racial groups than their own. The findings of the research are that a connection exists between these two viewpoints, and that connection will remain whichever way the statements are presented.

Q48   *Answer*: C.

Explanation: the passage does not comment on whether or not it is felt that racial tension has increased or decreased. Suggested answer C is clearly stated in the passage.

Q49   *Answer*: B.

Explanation: in the passage the terms community and neighbourhood are interchangeable and both are used to refer to the view that people pull together in their community.

Q50   *Answer*: D.

Explanation: suggested answer A is wrong because the passage is about the perception of racial tension not facts. B is wrong because the passage does not comment on whether or not the respondents live in communities with large ethnic minority communities. C is wrong because the passage states that people who had friends drawn from different racial groups felt there was less racial tension. It also states that people who thought their community pulled together felt there was less racial tension. However, the passage does not provide information on the question of whether or not people with friends from other racial groups also felt that their community pulled together, so D is correct.

Get super-numerate

Revise the basics
Addition

Q1   *Answer*: 10.
Q2   *Answer*: 15.
Q3   *Answer*: 13.
Q4   *Answer*: 12.
Q5   *Answer*: 14.
Q6   *Answer*: 13.
Q7   *Answer*: 12.
Q8   *Answer*: 10.
Q9   *Answer*: 13.
Q10 *Answer*: 11.
Q11 *Answer*: 23.
Q12 *Answer*: 27.
Q13 *Answer*: 31.
Q14 *Answer*: 25.
Q15 *Answer*: 33.
Q16 *Answer*: 30.
Q17 *Answer*: 32.
Q18 *Answer*: 36.
Q19 *Answer*: 31.
Q20 *Answer*: 39.
Q21 *Answer*: 689.
Q22 *Answer*: 859.
Q23 *Answer*: 999.
Q24 *Answer*: 634.
Q25 *Answer*: 931.

Q26 *Answer*: 872.

Q27 *Answer*: 960.

Q28 *Answer*: 1,493.

Q29 *Answer*: 1,142.

Q30 *Answer*: 1,711.

Sums that relate to the calculation of time

Q31 *Answer*: 57 minutes.

Q32 *Answer*: 1 hour 54 minutes.

Q33 *Answer*: 44 minutes.

Q34 *Answer*: 1 hour 55 minutes.

Q35 *Answer*: 1 hour 20 minutes.

Q36 *Answer*: 1 hour 46 minutes.

Q37 *Answer*: 1 hour.

Q38 *Answer*: 1 hour and 39 minutes.

Q39 *Answer*: 2 hours and 56 minutes.

Q40 *Answer*: 2 hours and 43 minutes.

Q41 *Answer*: 2 hours and 26 minutes.

Q42 *Answer*: 3 hours and 3 minutes.

Q43 *Answer*: 3 hours and 11 minutes.

Q44 *Answer*: 4 hours and 50 minutes.

Q45 *Answer*: 7 hours and 24 minutes.

Q46 *Answer*: 5 hours and 28 minutes.

Q47 *Answer*: 10 hours and 59 minutes.

Q48 *Answer*: 7 hours.

Q49 *Answer*: 12 hours and 7 minutes.

Q50 *Answer*: 9 hours and 12 minutes.

Subtraction

Q1 *Answer*: 1.

Q2 *Answer*: 6.

Q3 *Answer*: 7.

Q4 *Answer*: 8.

Q5 *Answer*: 6.

Q6 *Answer*: 8.

Q7 *Answer*: 8.

Q8 *Answer*: 12.
Q9 *Answer*: 9.
Q10 *Answer*: 13.
Q11 *Answer*: 113.
Q12 *Answer*: 160.
Q13 *Answer*: 241.
Q14 *Answer*: 691.
Q15 *Answer*: 213.
Q16 *Answer*: 149.
Q17 *Answer*: 150.
Q18 *Answer*: 536.
Q19 *Answer*: 91.
Q20 *Answer*: 187.
Q21 *Answer*: 49.
Q22 *Answer*: 275.
Q23 *Answer*: 249.
Q24 *Answer*: 195.
Q25 *Answer*: 368.
Q26 *Answer*: 437.
Q27 *Answer*: 335.
Q28 *Answer*: 138.
Q29 *Answer*: 414.
Q30 *Answer*: 89.

More sums that relate to the calculation of time

Q1 *Answer*: 28 minutes.
Q2 *Answer*: 14 minutes.
Q3 *Answer*: 7 minutes.
Q4 *Answer*: 13 minutes.
Q5 *Answer*: 6 minutes.
Q6 *Answer*: 1 hour 13 minutes.
Q7 *Answer*: 48 minutes.
Q8 *Answer*: 51 minutes.
Q9 *Answer*: 38 minutes.
Q10 *Answer*: 33 minutes.
Q11 *Answer*: 38 minutes.

Q12   *Answer*: 1 hour 22 minutes.
Q13   *Answer*: 53 minutes.
Q14   *Answer*: 14 minutes.
Q15   *Answer*: 55 minutes.
Q16   *Answer*: 25 minutes.
Q17   *Answer*: 3 hours 14 minutes.
Q18   *Answer*: 25 minutes.
Q19   *Answer*: 3 hours 34 minutes.
Q20   *Answer*: 4 minutes.
Q21   *Answer*: 3 hours 11 minutes.

Multiplication

Q1   *Answer*: 30.
Q2   *Answer*: 18.
Q3   *Answer*: 32.
Q4   *Answer*: 18.
Q5   *Answer*: 36.
Q6   *Answer*: 16.
Q7   *Answer*: 21.
Q8   *Answer*: 35.
Q9   *Answer*: 27.
Q10   *Answer*: 48.
Q11   *Answer*: 32.
Q12   *Answer*: 36.
Q13   *Answer*: 55.
Q14   *Answer*: 42.
Q15   *Answer*: 49.
Q16   *Answer*: 56.
Q17   *Answer*: 54.
Q18   *Answer*: 63.
Q19   *Answer*: 72.
Q20   *Answer*: 88.

Still more sums that relate to the calculation of time

Q1   *Answer*: 2 hours 40 minutes.
          Explanation: 20 × 8 = 160 = 2 hours and 40 minutes.

Q2   *Answer*: 1 hour and 12 minutes.
          Explanation: 4 × 18 = 72, 72 minutes = 1 hour and
          12 minutes.

Q3   *Answer*: 2 hours 45 minutes.
          Explanation: 55 × 3 = 165 minutes, which is 2 hours and
          45 minutes.

Q4   *Answer*: 8 hours and 30 minutes.
          Explanation: 30 × 17 = 510 minutes; 8 × 60 = 480 minutes
          so the answer is 8 hours and 30 minutes.

Q5   *Answer*: 1 hour 17 minutes.
          Explanation: 7 × 11 = 77; 77 – 60 = 17 so the answer is
          1 hour and 17 minutes.

Q6   *Answer*: 3 hours 18 minutes.
          Explanation: 22 × 9 = 198; 3 × 60 = 180 minutes so
          the answer is 3 hours 18 minutes.

Q7   *Answer*: 9 hours.
          Explanation: 90 × 6 = 540 = 9 hours.

Q8   *Answer*: 2 hours.
          Explanation: 24 × 5 = 120 = 2 hours.

Q9   *Answer*: 1 hour 36 minutes.
          Explanation: 12 × 8 = 96 minutes = 1 hour and 36 minutes.

Q10 *Answer*: 4 hours.
          Explanation: 20 × 12 = 240 = 4 hours.

Q11 *Answer*: 4 hours and 30 minutes.
          Explanation: 45 × 6 = 270 minutes = 4 hours and
          30 minutes.

Q12 *Answer*: 2 hours and 30 minutes.
          Explanation: 3 × 50 = 150 = 2 hours and 30 minutes.

Q13 *Answer*: 4 hours and 30 minutes.
          Explanation: 54 × 5 = 270 minutes = 4 hours and
          30 minutes.

Q14 *Answer*: 2 hours.
          Explanation: 8 × 15 = 120 = 2 hours.

Q15   *Answer*: 3 hours.
    Explanation: 18 × 10 = 180 = 3 hours.
Q16   *Answer*: 9 hours and 30 minutes.
    Explanation: 57 × 10 = 570 = 9 hours and 30 minutes.
Q17   *Answer*: 1 hour 48 minutes.
    Explanation: 18 × 6 = 108 minutes = 1 hour and
    48 minutes.
Q18   *Answer*: 5 hours and 30 minutes.
    Explanation: 10 × 33 = 330 = 5 hours and 30 minutes.
Q19   *Answer*: 1 hour and 36 minutes.
    Explanation: 24 × 4 = 96 minutes = 1 hour and 36 minutes.
Q20   *Answer*: 6 hours.
    Explanation: 120 × 3 = 360 = 6 hours.

Division and percentages

Q1   *Answer*: 4.
Q2   *Answer*: 12.5.
Q3   *Answer*: 7.
Q4   *Answer*: 9.
Q5   *Answer*: 9.
Q6   *Answer*: 5.
Q7   *Answer*: 3.
Q8   *Answer*: 9.
Q9   *Answer*: 12.
Q10   *Answer*: 9.
Q11   *Answer*: 5.
Q12   *Answer*: 8.
Q13   *Answer*: 5.
Q14   *Answer*: 4.
Q15   *Answer*: 14.
Q16   *Answer*: 6.
Q17   *Answer*: 5.
Q18   *Answer*: 6.
Q19   *Answer*: 15.
Q20   *Answer*: 4.
Q21   *Answer*: 21.
Q22   *Answer*: 15.

Q23   *Answer*: 2.5.
Q24   *Answer*: 15.
Q25   *Answer*: 21.
Q26   *Answer*: 25.
Q27   *Answer*: 12.
Q28   *Answer*: 2.5.
Q29   *Answer*: 240.
Q30   *Answer*: 72.
Q31   *Answer*: 0.01.
Q32   *Answer*: 480.
Q33   *Answer*: 1.
Q34   *Answer*: 0.25.
Q35   *Answer*: 350.
Q36   *Answer*: 0.1.
Q37   *Answer*: 0.6.
Q38   *Answer*: 0.5.
Q39   *Answer*: 0.005.
Q40   *Answer*: 0.9.
Q41   *Answer*: 100.
Q42   *Answer*: 0.4.
Q43   *Answer*: 420.
Q44   *Answer*: 12.
Q45   *Answer*: 13.5.
Q46   *Answer*: 0.04.
Q47   *Answer*: 8,800.
Q48   *Answer*: 5.
Q49   *Answer*: 48.
Q50   *Answer*: 30.

Using numbers and time

Situation 1

Q1   *Answer*: 26 minutes.
Q2   *Answer*: 26 minutes.
         Explanation: 41 minutes have passed from the time of the call to now, which leaves 26 minutes.

Q3 *Answer*: 6 minutes.

Q4 *Answer*: 10 minutes.

Q5 *Answer*: 12 minutes.

Q6 *Answer*: 10 minutes.

Q7 *Answer*: 55 minutes.

Q8 *Answer*: 24 minutes.

Q9 *Answer*: 8 minutes.

Q10 *Answer*: 1 minute.

Q11 *Answer*: 13 minutes.

Q12 *Answer*: 20 minutes.

Q13 *Answer*: 19 minutes.

Q14 *Answer*: 15 minutes.

Q15 *Answer*: 19 minutes.

More using numbers and time

Situation 2

Q1 Answer: 55 minutes.

Explanation: the crew left the station at 09.00 and took 15 minutes to reach the incident. They arrived at the incident therefore at 09.15. The time now is 10.10 so they have so far been at the incident for 55 minutes.

Q2 *Answer*: 50 minutes.

Q3 *Answer*: 93 minutes.

Q4 *Answer*: 18 minutes.

Q5 *Answer*: 32 minutes.

Q6 *Answer*: 64 minutes.

Q7 *Answer*: 68 minutes.

Q8 *Answer*: 15 minutes.

Q9 *Answer*: 28 minutes.

Q10 *Answer*: 66 minutes.

Q11 *Answer*: 44 minutes.

Q12 *Answer*: 25 minutes.

Q13 *Answer*: 74 minutes.

Q14 *Answer*: 1 minute.

Q15 *Answer*: 67 minutes.

Even more using numbers and time

Situation 3

Q1   *Answer*: 44 minutes.

Q2   *Answer*: 6 minutes.

Q3   *Answer*: 15 minutes.

Q4   *Answer*: 25 minutes.

Q5   *Answer*: 34 minutes.

Q6   *Answer*: 22 minutes.

Q7   *Answer*: 6 minutes.

Q8   *Answer*: 13 minutes.

Q9   *Answer*: 65 minutes.

Q10   *Answer*: 20 minutes.

Q11   *Answer*: 16 minutes.

Q12   *Answer*: none – time has run out.

Q13   *Answer*: 30 minutes.

Q14   *Answer*: 87 minutes.

Q15   *Answer*: 9 minutes.

Using numbers: other operations you must master

Q1   *Answer*: A.
Explanation: 50 multiplied by 75 = 3,750 m = 3.75 km.

Q2   *Answer*: C.
Explanation: to find the area of an oblong shape, multiply the length by the width. $6 \times 7 = 42$. The answer is 42 square metres and we signify this with the superscript 2: 42 m^2.

Q3   *Answer*: A.
Explanation: you need 60 m of hose to reach the storm drain and a further $20 + 10 = 30$ m to reach through the building and down the stairwell. You therefore need a total of 90 m of hose, so you require 9 lengths (each 10 m long).

Q4   *Answer*: C.
Explanation: each day Sam swims $30 \times 40 = 1,200$ m. Multiply this by 7 to get the total of 8.4 km.

Q5   *Answer*: A.

Explanation: a room occupying an area of 36 m² could have dimensions of any number of combinations, but of the suggested dimensions only answer A is correct. A room 9 m × 4 m would occupy an area of 36 m².

Q6   *Answer*: B.

Explanation: you have 15 × 20 = 300 m of hose if you connect all 20 lengths together. To establish how many floors up the tower block 300 m of hose will reach, divide 300 by the 18 m length of each floor. 300 ÷ 18 = 16 floors (12 m of hose is left but this is not enough to reach the 17th floor).

Q7   *Answer*: B.

Explanation: there are 60 minutes in an hour and Jo rows for 20 minutes, which is 1/3 of an hour (60 ÷ 20 = 3). To find the distance she covers, divide 18 km by a third to give you 6 km (6 × 3 = 18).

Q8   *Answer*: B.

Explanation: you can infer that he cycles seven days a week because the question states that he cycles every day, come rain or shine. To establish the daily average divide the weekly total by seven: 28 ÷ 7 = 4.

Q9   *Answer*: D.

Explanation: find the areas of each room and then total them. 6 × 6 = 36 + 7 × 7 = 49 + 4 × 3 = 12 = 97.

Q10   *Answer*: C.

Explanation: the distance from the fire to the hydrant is 90 + 30 + 16 = 136 m. Divide this by the 20 m lengths of hose. 136 ÷ 20 = 6.8; you will therefore need 7 lengths of hose.

Situation 1

Q11   *Answer*: A.

Explanation: in 2007 and 2006 combined, a total of 30 + 40 = 70 fatalities occurred. In 2005 there were a total of 50 fatalities. 70 – 50 = 20.

Q12 *Answer*: B.

Explanation: you must add all the figures for the two items over the three years. Injuries = 300 + 275 + 319; fatalities = 30 + 40 + 50; total = 1,014.

Q13 *Answer*: D.

Explanation: you find the answer by totalling the three annual figures for all emergencies and subtracting the total for the number of false alarms over the three years. All emergencies = 2,000 + 1,840 + 2,260 = 6,100 − (350 + 310 + 238) 898 = 5,202.

Q14 *Answer*: B.

Explanation: to find the area occupied by the seating we must calculate the area occupied by the whole auditorium and deduct the area occupied by the stage. To find the area occupied by the auditorium, multiply 14 × 12 = 168 and subtract 64 to find the area occupied by the seating alone = 104 m^2.

Q15 *Answer*: C.

Explanation: 3 km = 3,000 m and 3,000 ÷ 120 = 25 m, so Jack swims 25 m a length. He has 2 km still to go and 2 km = 2,000 m ÷ 25 = 80 lengths still to go.

Q16 *Answer*: B.

Explanation: you are told that the land is square in shape and therefore you can assume that all sides are of equal length. The area occupied by the piece of land therefore is 14 × 14 = 196 m^2; add this to the area occupied by the lake and you get the total 666 m^2.

Situation 2

Q17 *Answer*: B.

Explanation: the total number of people in the survey from your neighbourhood = 900 and you can estimate from the pie chart that a quarter of these are aged over 60. 900 ÷ 4 = 225, which falls within range B.

Q18   *Answer*: C.

Explanation: to find the total for the two age groups (0–17 and 18–59) you simply combine the totals for those groups: 25,000 + 50,000 = 75,000.

Q19   *Answer*: C.

Explanation: it is clear from the pie chart of your neighbourhood that half of the population is aged between 18–59 years. It is also clear from the bar chart for the city overall that 50,000 people from a total of 100,000 (= half) of the people are of that age.

Q20   *Answer*: B.

Explanation: you must run the hose a total distance of 9 × 8 m = 72 m. The lengths of hose are 30 metres, so you will need 3 (2 lengths would only reach 60 m).

Q21   *Answer*: D.

Explanation: 4 km = 4,000 m. To discover the length of the pool we must divide 4,000 by the number of lengths: 4,000 ÷ 50 = 80.

Situation 3

Q22   *Answer*: A.

Explanation: to find the total number of accidents attended, add the three subtotals 35 + 30 + 50 = 115.

Q23   *Answer*: D.

Explanation: there were 50 summer incidents and 40 winter incidents, so the service attended 10 more incidents in the summer.

Q24   *Answer*: D.

Explanation: A is untrue because motorways appear safest in the summer not spring, and B is untrue because more accidents involving pedestrians occur in the spring and winter combined, so the majority do not occur in the summer. C is untrue because the service attends 115 motorway accidents and 120 accidents in 20-mile zones. D is true because the number of incidents in the spring totals 65 while summer = 80 and winter 90.

Q25   *Answer*: C.

Explanation: 10 × 15 = 150. You have 150 m of hose, and need 20 m for each storey. 150 ÷ 20 = 7.5.

Q26   *Answer*: C.

Explanation: Jane runs at 16 km an hour (which = 16 km in 60 minutes) for 15 minutes. 15 minutes = 1/4 of an hour (60 ÷ 15 = 4) so she would cover 16 ÷ 4 = 4 km in each 15-minute session. To cover 40 km would therefore take her 10 sessions.

Situation 4

Q27   *Answer*: C.

Explanation: find this total by adding the night and daytime figures for kitchen fires. 200 + 350 = 550.

Q28   *Answer*: B.

Explanation: find this by adding all the night and daytime figures for household fires in Scotland. 90 + 75 + 87 + 70 + 150 + 40 + 50 + 30 = 592.

Q29   *Answer*: D.

Explanation: first add the night and daytime subtotal for kitchen fires in Scotland to find the total kitchen fires in Scotland = 240. Divide this by 3 = 80 fires caused by washing machines, leaving 160 (240 – 80) kitchen fires in Scotland caused by things other than washing machines.

Q30   *Answer*: C.

Explanation: you have a total of 5 × 30 m of hose = 150 m; divide this total by 20 to find the number of floors you can reach: 150 ÷ 20 = 7.5. This means that you would reach the 7th floor or storey of the tower but not the 8th.

Q31   *Answer*: D.

Explanation: the key to the answer to this question is that it is stated that half the roof of the warehouse has collapsed and the size of hole of the roof is given. With this information you can calculate the area occupied by the warehouse because it will be twice the size of the hole in the roof. So calculate 40 × 150 = 6,000 × 2 = 12,000.

Q32   *Answer*: B.

Explanation: there are six of you (you and five colleagues) each Sunday; therefore you run a total of 30 km and in 10 Sundays you would cover 300 km.

Situation 5

Q33   *Answer*: C.

Explanation: the figure is found by totalling the three annual figures found on the graph titled 'All reported fires'. The scale of this graph is given as '000s', which means 10 = 10,000, 20 = 20,000 and so on. So 2007 = 10,000 + 20,000 (2005) + 30,000 (2006) = 60,000 fires.

Q34   *Answer*: B.

Explanation: find the figure by adding the figure for fires attributed to arson in which a fatality did not occur and fires attributed to arson in which a fatality did occur. The first of these graphs totals 700 fires (100 (2007) + 200 (2006) + 400 (2005)). The second totals 60. This gives a grand total of 760.

Q35   *Answer*: A.

Explanation: we can find the figure if we subtract the number of fires attributed to arson from all reported fires. 60,000 − 760 = 59,240.

Q36   *Answer*: C.

Explanation: you have 6 × 20 lengths of hose = 120 m. Divide this by the 15 m you require for each floor and the answer is 8 floors.

Q37   *Answer*: D.

Explanation: you must add the full marathon, 26 miles, + the two half marathons + the 1/3. 1/3 of 26 = 8.66, so the total = 26 + 13 + 13 + 8.66 = over 60 miles.

Situation 6

Q38   *Answer*: B.

Explanation: the figure can be read straight from the second graph. Note the scale of this graph is in '00s' = 100s, so 9 (00s) = 900.

Q39 *Answer*: A.

Explanation: to find the answer you must total the figures for both men and women aged under and over 60 years. These figures are: over 60 years 2,000 men, 1,000 women; under 60 years 700 men and 600 women. This gives a grand total of 4,300.

Q40 *Answer*: C.

Explanation: in Germany 4,000 men and 3,000 women over 60 suffer a fire in their home = 7,000. In France 2,000 men and 2,000 women over 60 suffer a fire. Therefore 3,000 more people in Germany than France aged over 60 who live alone suffer a fire in their home.

The situational awareness paper

The first 26 situational questions – answers

Q1 *Answer*

1	2	3	4
B	C	B	B

Explanation: rumours have no place at work. They distract everyone from performing their expected duties, resulting in a less productive work day, cause unnecessary conflict and are detrimental to employee relations and morale. Suggested responses 1, 3 and 4 would help stop the rumour, so are acceptable responses. Suggested response 2 would not help stop it, so is a less than acceptable response.

Q2 *Answer*

1	2	3	4
C	C	B	B

Explanation: race discrimination occurs when a person is treated less favourably on the grounds of race, colour, nationality, ethnic or national origin. It is unlawful to practise racial discrimination. Your employer is responsible for ensuring that there is no racism in the workplace. Colleagues who knowingly discriminate against another employee on the grounds of race, or who aid discriminatory practices, are also acting unlawfully. Suggested response 1 is less than acceptable because it is only concerned with the name calling and not the other forms of discrimination described in the passage. Suggested response 2 is also less than acceptable because in the passage you are described as the only black employee, so you can't talk to colleagues who might be suffering the same problems. Suggested responses 3 and 4 are both acceptable because they might end the discrimination. Neither of the responses in isolation is the most appropriate response because it would be better if you did both and kept a record of the instances as well as using an official grievance procedure to give your employer the chance to stop it.

Q3   *Answer*

1	2	3	4
C	C	C	A

Explanation: whatever the size of the business, your employer has a duty of care to look after your health, safety and welfare while you are at work. This duty of care includes making sure that ventilation, temperature and lighting, and toilet, washing and rest facilities all meet health, safety and welfare requirements. This includes providing somewhere for employees to get changed and to store their own clothes and an area set aside for rest breaks and to eat meals, including if necessary suitable facilities for pregnant women and nursing mothers. Response 1 is less than acceptable because you have tried this before and it has failed. Response 2 is less than acceptable because it is not the case that a small business does not have a duty of care for its employees. Suggested response 3 is also less than acceptable because a tribunal would expect you to have raised the matter formally with your employer. Response 4 is the most acceptable because you have tried to resolve the issue informally and failed, and it is therefore proper that you raise the matter formally.

Q4   *Answer*

1	2	3	4
A	C	C	B

Explanation: you should first try to resolve disagreements with co-workers informally, but if this fails and despite the passing of time the matter continues then you should involve your supervisor or manager to see if they can resolve matters. If neither of these actions works and the issue continues to affect your work then you should take the matter up formally. Do this using your employer's formal procedures for grievances. You should be able to find these in either your company's handbook or as an appendix to your contract of employment. Suggested response 1 is the most appropriate because it seeks to resolve the matter informally between the workers involved and then seeks to resolve it informally with the supervisor. Responses 2 and 3 do not follow the recommended procedure so are less than acceptable. Suggested response 4 is acceptable but it is not the most appropriate because it does not try to resolve things informally with your co-workers first before involving management.

Q5   *Answer*

1	2	3	4
C	C	A	C

Explanation: if a firefighter were to steal from an incident it would constitute a serious breach of trust. Firefighters attend to, for example, people's homes and businesses when they have been abandoned, leaving property behind. A firefighter who helped himself to that property would be committing a serious criminal offence and it would be the duty of any witness to report that crime. For this reason suggested response 1 and 2 are less than acceptable. Response 3 is the most appropriate because it would ensure that the matter was dealt with immediately. Response 4 would be less than acceptable because it would allow the individual time to dispose of the money and deny everything.

Q6   *Answer*

1	2	3	4
B	A	B	C

Explanation: if the job that your wife had wanted to apply for had been in a call-centre, for example, then good spoken English would be a reasonable requirement. However it is not a reasonable requirement for a job on a production line. We all have a responsibility to challenge what we consider amounts to unfair discrimination. So do contact the people behind something that you consider racist or discriminatory and politely explain your objection. Responses 1 and 3 are acceptable because they amount to actions that will question and challenge what may well be indirect discrimination. Response 2 is the most appropriate because if the employers agree then it means your wife has not missed out on an opportunity despite a misleading advertisement. Response C is less than acceptable because it fails to challenge what might be discriminatory practice.

Q7   *Answer*

1	2	3	4
B	C	C	B

Explanation: your employer should have systems and procedures in place to minimize the risk of pressures that create stress. When a member of staff falls ill due to stress at work then employers should review the person's role and look at ways to remove the causes of the stress and ill health. If you write to them informing them of a stress-related illness, then they should respond by offering to meet with you and discuss ways to help you return to work and avoid the risk of the illness reoccurring. Responses 1 and 4 would allow the employer the opportunity to meet their responsibility to adjust your workload and provide a healthy place of work and so are both acceptable. Both responses 2 and 3 are less than acceptable. Response 2 is less than acceptable because the illness was due to the amount of work and not a lack of lunch breaks or extra hours worked. Response 3 is less than acceptable because it does not seek to address your workload, which is the cause of your ill health.

Q8   *Answer*

1	2	3	4
B	C	C	A

Explanation: you can expect your boss to be able to listen to someone distressed and be able to recognize signs of stress and have some understanding of possible ill-health outcomes. It is reasonable to expect your employer to have the systems and procedures in place to minimize the risk of pressures creating stress and leading to ill health, and to be able to accommodate events such as a bereavement by making adjustments to workloads. Suggested response 1 is acceptable but more is needed before it can be described as the most appropriate. Suggested responses 2 and 3 are less than acceptable because they do not secure the change necessary for you cope with your return to work. Suggested response 4 is the most appropriate because it is likely to reduce the pressures on you.

Q9   *Answer*

1	2	3	4
C	C	C	A

Explanation: we all make mistakes, even ones that make us feel extremely foolish. An employer can expect to be informed of your mistakes at the earliest opportunity. Only suggested response 4 is acceptable because all other suggested responses fail to inform your employer at the time of the loss. Imagine if you were to follow suggested response 1 and proceed to the next station to discover that the item had not been found on the train? You would then have to phone your employer and explain that you had left the item, did not report the loss and went to the next station only to find that it was not there.

Q10 *Answer*

1	2	3	4
B	C	A	C

Explanation: your employers are probably trying to grapple with legal and business continuity issues. The work environment described in the situation sounds like a very difficult place and senior management would be trying to resolve it. It would not be right under the circumstances to discuss the matter directly with your manager, but it is equally not appropriate that you put up with it because it is affecting your work and upsetting you. The more appropriate responses are responses 1 and 3 because they will ensure that management are informed of the additional problems and so can do something about them. Suggested response 3 is the most appropriate because of the professional and empathetic approach adopted.

Q11 *Answer*

1	2	3	4
B	C	C	B

Explanation: we all have a duty to challenge sexism when we hear it. The fact that the discriminatory term is only used outside work makes no difference to that responsibility. Responses 2 and 3 fail to live up to that responsibility and so are less than acceptable. Responses 1 and 4 challenge it and so are equally appropriate.

Q12 *Answer*

1	2	3	4
C	C	A	C

Explanation: a firefighter must respect the confidentiality of the victims and their family. The fact that the newspapers or other media are covering the event does not change the duty to maintain that confidentiality. Only suggested response 3 is acceptable because it upholds that confidentially of the victims. Yes it helps to talk about distressing events, but a firefighter must be very careful with whom he or she holds those conversations. Firefighters can always contact HR and ask to speak to a welfare officer if they are finding it difficult to come to terms with something that they have witnessed.

Q13 *Answer*

1	2	3	4
B	C	B	A

Explanation: suggested response 4 is the most appropriate because it proposes a practical way in which the open days can be made more accessible to a wider number of members of the community. Suggested responses 1 and 3 are acceptable but response 1 lacks any practical suggestions and response 3 only addresses the problem encountered with the community elder on the day. Response 2 is less than acceptable because it fails to achieve the objective of an open day, which is to make the fire station accessible to all members of the community.

Q14 *Answer*

1	2	3	4
C	C	A	C

Explanation: responses 1, 2 and 4 only re-communicate the assigned roles and do not allow for the possibility that the assignment of roles could be improved or that duplication or conflict of roles since the reorganization may be the cause of the tension between the workers. Response 3 is the most appropriate because it seeks the views of the individuals concerned as well as reviewing the assignment of roles.

Q15 *Answer*

1	2	3	4
A	C	C	C

Explanation: this is a serious matter and response 1 is the most appropriate given that a theft has occurred. Responses 2 and 4 are less than appropriate because they do not attribute sufficient importance or seriousness to the situation. Response 3 is less than appropriate because you may not have the authority to search the personal property of other members of staff. It would be better to leave that to the police.

Q16 *Answer*

1	2	3	4
B	C	C	A

Explanation: response 1 is acceptable but may risk inflaming the situation so is not therefore necessarily the most appropriate approach. Responses 2 and 3 are both less than acceptable because they do not prevent the person from using further bad language. Response 4 is the most appropriate because it both prevents further bad language and avoids any further risk of inflaming the situation by explaining that you wish to apologize.

Q17 *Answer*

1	2	3	4
C	A	B	C

Explanation: response 1 is less than acceptable because a threat of violence is a serious matter that cannot be ignored. Response 2 is the most appropriate because it will guarantee that the matter is dealt with according to the correct procedure. Response 3 is an acceptable response because it will ensure that the matter is dealt with by management. Response 4 is less than acceptable because it would be unreasonable to expect the person threatened to have to resolve the matter him/herself without the support of management.

Q18 *Answer*

1	2	3	4
C	C	C	A

Explanation: response 4 is the most appropriate approach because it will address the issue in a confidential and appropriate manner. Response 1 is less than acceptable because it involves the disclosure of personal details to a colleague. Response 2 is less than acceptable because a team meeting is not a suitable event in which to discuss with an individual a matter such as body odour. Response 3 is less than acceptable because the fact that someone else has also noticed the problem means that you can no longer ignore the situation.

Q19 *Answer*

1	2	3	4
B	C	B	B

Explanation: if there is bullying of any kind, or other behaviour that affects your health or ability to do your job, then a good employer will make changes to stop it. No employer should tolerate bullying of any kind, and especially not of the sort described in this situation. If they cannot resolve it informally then they should initiate disciplinary action against any harasser. If your employer does not take action against such an individual then you may be able to use the law to make them change their approach. Responses 1, 3 and 4 are acceptable responses because they support the individuals affected and should lead to a resolution. Response 2 is less than acceptable because it is unlikely to result in a resolution.

Q20 *Answer*

1	2	3	4
C	C	B	A

Explanation: if you are left feeling speechless and upset then it is not acceptable (as suggested in response 1) that nothing can be done about it and that you must just carry on and do your job as professionally as possible. The kind of behaviour demonstrated by the person in the situation is completely unacceptable and we all have a responsibility to challenge it and help stop it. Responses 3 and 4 are likely to result in her modifying her behaviour. Response 4 is the best response because it is most likely to ensure the situation does not reoccur. Response 2 is less than acceptable because it is very likely to make matters worse as it is stated in the passage that trying to reason with her makes her even more aggressive.

Q21   *Answer*

1	2	3	4
C	B	C	C

Explanation: response 1 is less than acceptable because while it is correct that the perpetrator should be challenged it would be wrong to call someone an idiot. Responses 3 and 4 are also less than acceptable because the fact that the event happened outside work does not mean that a code of conduct does not apply or that we have to accept inappropriate banter. Response 2 is appropriate in that it will result in supporting Jane; however it is not the best possible response because it fails to challenge the behaviour of the perpetrator (which should be done in a non-confrontational way).

Q22   *Answer*

1	2	3	4
C	C	B	A

Explanation: response 1 is less than acceptable because if you are discontented in your work you should raise it with management. It is also less than acceptable to go and look for another job when you have not given your manager the chance to put matters right. Response 3 is acceptable but it focuses on the negative and, unlike response 4, fails to offer a constructive suggestion as to how the situation could be improved.

Q23 *Answer*

1	2	3	4
C	C	B	A

Explanation: response 1 is less than acceptable because, while you may feel that you have received enough instruction to operate the crusher, it is the employer's responsibility to ensure that training and instruction is sufficient to ensure the safety of workers. Response 2 is also less than acceptable because an employer should not instruct you to operate equipment without proper instruction and or training, and this is irrespective of the number of employees. Response 3 is acceptable but the best approach is response 4 because, while you decline to operate the machinery, you explain why and this gives the employer the opportunity to arrange the necessary instruction so that you can carry out your duties safely.

Q24 *Answer*

1	2	3	4
A	C	C	B

Explanation: response 1 is the best approach, given that you have tried and failed to resolve the matter informally, and your watch leader is the most appropriate person to involve next. It may well be that your watch leader can ban all further discussion of the subject and advise Paul that he must stop. Response 2 is unlikely to succeed because such an approach has already been tried and failed, so it is less than acceptable. Response 3 is less than acceptable because it does not seek to resolve the problem. You might escape the problem but you will leave your colleagues to have to deal with it. Response 4 is acceptable in that it is reasonable that you approach a personnel officer; however it would be better if you first took the issue to your watch leader, and approach personnel only if he or she is unable to resolve the matter.

Q25 *Answer*

1	2	3	4
C	C	A	C

Explanation: personal issues, including family problems and emotional difficulties, do sometimes impact on your work. Try as you might to keep your private life separate from your work life, inevitably when the personal issues are a great as those described in the passage, one often runs into the other. In these circumstances you have no practical alternative but to inform your manager of the difficulties and request that they accommodate your situation wherever practical. Responses 1, 2 and 3 are all less than acceptable because they do not acknowledge the fact that your personal problems are impacting on your working life. Response 4 is the most appropriate because it acknowledges the impact of your personal problems on your work and seeks to deal with it.

Q26 *Answer*

1	2	3	4
C	B	B	C

Explanation: response 1 is less than acceptable. Your weight has increased by 8 or 9 kg in the last two years and to change nothing will mean that this trend is very likely to continue. That will mean that at some point your weight will impact on your ability to do your job. Response 4 is also less than acceptable because it is unlikely to succeed. The situation describes how your family commitments mean that you no longer have the time to go to the gym or run, so unless you involve others in your plan it is very likely that you will continue to have insufficient time to exercise. Responses 2 and 3 are both acceptable because either may well give you the support you need in order to come to terms with your weight gain and correct it.

Thirteen questions to get you thinking about priorities and getting them in the order that the Fire Service expects

Q1 *Answer*: C.

Explanation: a firefighter's priorities are to save life, prevent injury and protect property. A person in danger of death or injury would obviously be assisted before a dog. However, a drowning dog will die if not given immediate assistance and none of the other situations involves a risk of death or injury.

Q2 *Answer*: B.

Explanation: firefighters face many dangerous situations and continue to carry out instructions both when they are tired and when a situation is getting worse.

Q3 *Answer*: D.

Explanation: when faced with a fire, we would first raise the alarm and help evacuate the building. Before we fought a fire we would assess the risk of its spread and growth so that we do not become trapped or overcome by heat or smoke.

Q4 *Answer*: A.

Explanation: the trapped man is at great risk of death caused by the rising flood water and so we should help him before the others.

Q5 *Answer*: C.

Explanation: the situations described at A, B and D are all very urgent. You would need to act immediately and do not have the time to request permission before you acted. The situation described at C is not so urgent and you would need to request permission before you left your post evacuating people.

Q6 *Answer*: B.

Explanation: when organizing an evacuation you would first estimate the number of people to be evacuated. You are then in a position to (second) identify an adequate means of escape, start the evacuation and assist anyone who needs it.

Q7 *Answer*: D.

Explanation: firefighting unavoidably involves risks that potentially could cause the death of a firefighter. These risks are kept to a minimum and are only taken if the situation requires it. Firefighters will not take such risks to recover property nor will they take such risks to recover a dead body. They will, however, risk their lives to rescue a colleague or homeless person, and even someone who is trying to commit suicide.

Q8 *Answer*: B.

Explanation: situations A and C involve important information that could have a significant bearing on the safety of the people involved and so should be reported immediately. Situation D should also be reported because the property must be returned to its owner. Only situation B would not need to be reported.

Q9 *Answer*: D.

Explanation: fire D involves the risk of death or injury to people (the fact that those people are terminally ill is irrelevant). The warehouse is described as deserted, the fire in the school has occurred in the early hours (which means after midnight but still at night) and so the school will be empty. Smoke blowing across the town is a danger and could cause injury but is less urgent than fire D.

Q10 *Answer*: A.

Explanation: the priorities of the Fire Service are life, injury and property. So if presented with the described situation the firefighter would recover the property last, having first helped the elderly person to safety, rescued the animal and put out the fire.

Q11 *Answer*: B.

Explanation: a firefighter would be most concerned with the prevention of death or injury and damage to property. Given these priorities situation B would give rise to most concern as there is a risk of injury unless the tree is removed.

Q12 *Answer*: D.

Explanation: firefighters take risks and worry about them in the sense that they take them seriously. A delay in reaching an emergency would worry a firefighter because it might lead to a greater risk to life or property. Everyone makes mistakes and we should not worry about reporting them immediately to someone in authority.

Q13 *Answer*: C.

Explanation: in situation D you would need to leave the scene immediately (help might involve a greater risk to you and your helpers' lives if your only means of escape is lost). Situation B would be unfortunate but would not require urgent help. This leaves situations A and C. Both require immediate help and you must decide which is most urgent. It is a close call but situation C is more urgent because of the high risk of further injury or loss of life that could occur if one of the passing vehicles was to collide with the crushed car on which you are working.

Seven questions in the format found in the real situations awareness paper

Q14 *Answer*: A.

Explanation: you have been asked to promote the business case for fire safety training; there is no mention of, for example, any legal duty or of the lethal effects of a fire. Only suggested answer A properly follows the instruction.

Q15 *Answer*: D.

Explanation: when you are working as part of a team it is usually possible to address more than one pressing priority at a time. Answer D is the best response because it is essential you immediately establish if anyone is still in the submerged vehicle but also provide assistance to the injured until the ambulance service arrives. Extra assistance is required because the incident involves casualties and more vehicles than reported, as well as the complication of vehicles down an embankment.

Q16 *Answer*: B.

Explanation: even though you were told to collect the goods when you had finished your lunch break, the fact that it looks as if it might start raining again any minute means it would be better if you collected the goods immediately so as to avoid any risk of them getting spoiled by the rain.

Q17 *Answer*: C.

Explanation: only one member of the team needs to stop working for a short while in order to establish what the person has to say and this would not delay the completion of the job to any significant extent. The person may be approaching to say something urgent, or may require some information regarding fire safety. It is far better that they are treated courteously and given a few minutes full attention, which would not be the case if you continued working while listening to them.

Q18 *Answer*: D.

Explanation: of the suggested answers, D is preferable. Options A and C would be inappropriate as Tom could easily end up being burned to death while inebriated. It is not the role of the Fire Service to remove someone from what is in effect their 'home' and ban them from returning. This leaves option D as the best suggestion.

Q19 *Answer*: A.

Explanation: this is a question of priorities. The Fire Service will first act to save life or prevent injury and will save property second, irrespective of its value. The scenario describes the building as large, so splitting the team would risk your not finding the night watchman before the fire took too great a hold.

Q20 *Answer*: D.

Explanation: firefighters have a duty to maintain their fitness throughout their career so suggested answer A is not acceptable. It is far better to be proactive and make constructive suggestions, as done in answer D, than complain or expect someone else to find the answer as implied in suggested answers B and C.

A practice situational awareness and problem solving test

Q1   *Answer*: C.

Explanation: someone is calling for help and may be in grave danger. Your colleague is hurt but not so badly that he cannot be left while you assess the situation.

Q2   *Answer*: B.

Explanation: the role of the Fire Service is to save life, prevent injury and protect property (in that order). It is the responsibility of the police to apprehend arsonists.

Q3   *Answer*: D.

Explanation: the situation is described as critical and this calls for urgent action. It is better to save the person's life, even if it means their legs and feet get knocked and bruised, than to leave them or delay the evacuation by waiting. You are one of a team of seven and there are a dozen people who need carrying to the surface, so if two of you carry the person it will mean someone else has to wait behind unassisted.

Q4   *Answer*: D.

Explanation: if you inadvertently upset someone, the thing to do is apologize.

Q5   *Answer*: A.

Explanation: the senior firefighter knows that the canisters are on the premises and so you can safely assume he has made an assessment of the situation and decided it is a necessary and manageable risk. The senior firefighter will have decided the job requires two people and that you and your colleague are best suited for the task.

Q6   *Answer*: B.

Explanation: it is better that you get some help and get the job finished on time than complete the job late or badly or leave it uncompleted.

Q7   *Answer*: D.

Explanation: there is no time to reason with the person and insistence alone may not succeed. D is a better response than C because he may do as he is told.

Q8 *Answer*: C.

Explanation: you have been asked to tell him something imperative; this means urgent and critical and it is safe to assume that it cannot wait.

Q9 *Answer*: A.

Explanation: the news is a surprise to you and most likely to the officer in charge too. You should inform him immediately and allow him to decide if the information changes his decision about the most appropriate action.

Q10 *Answer*: A.

Explanation: if your private life is affecting your work then it does become your employer's business. The scenario states that you have already tried to segregate your work and private life, so it is unlikely that greater resolve to keep them separate will improve the situation. You should be honest with your line manager and you can expect her, where practical, to temporarily reorganize things to better accommodate your difficulties.

Q11 *Answer*: D.

Explanation: you would move the vehicle manually because you would not want the fire engine damaged if that meant you were not able to proceed to the emergency.

Q12 *Answer*: C.

Explanation: the Fire Service works hard to promote itself to every section of society, and racist graffiti close to the station could undermine that good work. The longer the graffiti remains the more chance there is of offence being caused, and to remove it immediately would demonstrate commendable initiative.

Q13 *Answer*: B.

Explanation: it would be unwise to ignore how you feel, because in an emergency situation this could endanger your or a colleague's life. It would be best to go along but inform the officer in charge at the first opportunity. That way you are not delaying the response.

Q14   *Answer*: B.

Explanation: it would not take any more time to make a very brief apology such as 'excuse me' before you left, and this would be preferable to option C where you say nothing.

Q15   *Answer*: C.

Explanation: the scenario does not detail the correct action to take in the situation described. For this reason you should select suggested answer C and immediately report your find to your line manager so that he or she may initiate the correct response.

Q16   *Answer*: D.

Explanation: no employer would want a member of staff who was not responsible for the purchase of goods to enter into an agreement to buy something. The best action in such circumstances would be to take details and propose the idea.

Q17   *Answer*: D.

Explanation: the issue involves public safety and so should not be left until next year or until you arrive back from leave. However, it is not so urgent that it cannot wait until tomorrow, so you should not trouble your manager at home but instead phone the station the next day.

Q18   *Answer*: C.

Explanation: in an emergency situation there may not always be enough time to seek permission or instructions before you act, and in these circumstances it is best to take action and report it as soon as it is practical to do so.

Q19   *Answer*: A.

Explanation: in the situation your team is described as working frantically to extract a badly injured person. For this reason you cannot spare a member of your team to investigate the other incident nor can you delay the extraction. The police are at the incident and they may be able to investigate the other accident. You should complete the extraction first and then go to the assistance of anyone hurt in the other incident.

Q20   *Answer*: D.

   Explanation: of the four possible responses, the option of telling people that they should stop is the best. Were they still to continue or if you preferred not to confront your new colleagues, then you would need to inform your manager of the situation, and you could then expect him or her to ensure that the remarks cease.

Fault diagnosis

Ten input type questions

Q1   *Answer*: D.

   Explanation: the first change deletes the K, next the U is changed to V and finally a P is inserted between the Z and L.

Q2   *Answer*: A.

   Explanation: the first change deletes the P, then the N is replaced with an M and finally the C and the first M are exchanged.

Q3   *Answer*: C.

   Explanation: the A become B, then the sequence is reversed to become RDEGBUG and finally the B becomes a C.

Q4   *Answer*: B.

   Explanation: first the S is deleted, then a P is inserted between the A and the first T, and finally we replace the first T with a U.

Q5   *Answer*: C.

   Explanation: the first rule deletes the E, then the second I is replaced with a J and finally the sequence is reversed to read DJTION.

Q6   *Answer*: D.

Q7   *Answer*: B.

Q8   *Answer*: C.

Q9   *Answer*: A.

Q10   *Answer*: D.

Spatial recognition and visual estimation

Q11 *Answer*: C.

Explanation: a) shows the right side b) shows the left side.

Q12 *Answer*: C.

Explanation: a) shows the left side b) shows the right side.

Q13 *Answer*: A.

Explanation: in b) the middle part is too long, and c) has too many edges (count them and compare with the original).

Q14 *Answer*: B.

Explanation: a) shows the right side, and c) shows the left side.

Q15 *Answer*: A.

Explanation: all you can see from above is the three steps; in b) this zigzag form is not part of the original, and c) shows the right side.

Q16 *Answer*: B.

Explanation: in a) the small 'roof' shape has been moved, in c) the small 'roof' shape is missing, and in d) the central part of the shape is too small.

Q17 *Answer*: A.

Explanation: b) is wrong because it represents an extruded irregular quadrangle, in c) the shape has been shortened, and in d) the shape has been lengthened.

Q18 *Answer*: D.

Explanation: in a), b) and c) the rectangular shape has been moved.

Q19 *Answer*: B.

Explanation: it is the only one with a 'roof' on the intersection of the 'L'-shape.

Q20 *Answer*: A.

Explanation: b) has a 'W' shape instead of a 'T' shape, and c) has a 'Z' shape instead of a 'T' shape.

Q21 *Answer*: C.

Explanation: in a) the triangular shape has been deformed, and in b) and d) the cube has been deformed.

Q22   *Answer*: D.
Explanation: in a) the big triangular shape has been thickened, in b) the big triangular shape has been thinned, and in c) the small triangular shape has been deformed.

Q23   *Answer*: B.
Explanation: in a) and c) the right triangular shape has been truncated; in d) both triangular shapes have had the edges cut off.

Q24   *Answer*: B.
Explanation: in a) and c) the small cube has been moved.

Q25   *Answer*: A.
Explanation: in b) and c) the hexagonal shape has been deformed.

Chapter 4, Practice tests

Practice test 1

Q1   *Answer*: C.
Explanation: the passage states that some businesses fail to recover, not that a business is unlikely to recover, so the correct answer is C (may not recover). The reference in the passage to many millions of pounds refers to the total cost each year to business, not the losses of a single business if a fire occurs.

Q2   *Answer*: A.
Explanation: the passage states that fire may grow unexpectedly fast and this can be correctly rephrased as grow at an alarming rate. Fires do produce smoke and heat and can burn unnoticed, but these points are not made in the passage.

Q3   *Answer*: C.
Explanation: the passage states that the potential for an accidental fire exists in a large number of everyday activities, and no doubt these include all the suggested answers. But the question asks which activity the passage

specifically states, and of the suggested answers only driving a car is specifically mentioned.

Q4   *Answer*: D.

Explanation: the opening line of the passage states 'We can all recognize fire but the majority of us fail to fully understand it.'

Q5   *Answer*: B.

Explanation: the passage states that every year people are killed, and even more are injured, by fires that occur in the workplace, whilst travelling and in the home.

Q6   *Answer*: A.

Explanation: the passage makes a strong business case for ensuring that staff know what to do in the event of a fire and points out that there is a legal obligation too.

Q7   *Answer*: A.

Explanation: the passage describes two precautions that could save a business from having to face the devastating effects of an accidental fire. Another way to describe a precaution is safety measure, and of the suggested answers, A best represents what is said in the passage.

Q8   *Answer*: B.

Explanation: the passage states that most employers must provide adequate training in fire awareness.

Q9   *Answer*: D.

Explanation: the passage states that their workforce is trained to the very highest standards.

Q10   *Answer*: C.

Explanation: the passage does not say whether or not employers can or should be prosecuted if they fail to provide fire safety training, so you can reject suggested answers A and B on this basis. Given that the first line of the passage states 'every business should ensure that employees know what to do in the event of a fire', you can identify suggested answer C as a better restatement of the sentiment of the passage than suggested answer D.

Q11   *Answer*: B.

Explanation: the passage states only that many fires start at night when the occupants are asleep, and this can be rephrased as being common at night. No mention is made in the passage regarding the frequency of fires that start during the day or whether they are more common at night.

Q12   *Answer*: A.

Explanation: that suggested answer A is correct can be inferred from the passage, which says that all electric appliances not designed to be on all the time should be switched off and unplugged, and later describes washing machines as appliances not designed to be on all the time.

Q13   *Answer*: D.

Explanation: the passage states that if you have an open fire you should always use a spark guard.

Q14   *Answer*: D.

Explanation: the passage states that 'So many fires in the home start at night when the occupants are asleep that everyone should follow a fire safety routine before they go to bed.' And everybody is another way of saying everyone.

Q15   *Answer*: C.

Explanation: C is another way of stating what is said in the passage, namely that you should 'close all doors throughout your property as this will slow down the spread of any heat or smoke generated by a fire'.

Q16   *Answer*: B.

Explanation: the passage states that smoke alarms are useless without a battery or if the battery is flat. The passage also describes a type of smoke alarm suitable for people who have difficulty hearing.

Q17   *Answer*: A.

Explanation: the passage states that ideally you should fit them in every room except the bedrooms.

Q18   *Answer*: C.

Explanation: the passage does not contain any comment about vacuuming a smoke alarm monthly or once a year, only from time to time.

Q19   *Answer*: D.

Explanation: the passage describes special smoke alarms for people who have difficulty hearing, and this is a disability.

Q20   *Answer*: B.

Explanation: suggested answer B is an accurate summary of the passage, which states in the opening sentence that fitting a smoke alarm could save lives.

Q21   *Answer*: D.

Explanation: the passage states that the findings (ie conclusions) of a fire-risk assessment must be recorded.

Q22   *Answer*: B.

Explanation: the passage states that most employers are required by law to do this.

Q23   *Answer*: C.

Explanation: the passage states that a fire safety inspecting officer can prohibit the use of a part or all of a building with immediate effect if he or she thinks it is unsafe, and prohibit means stop.

Q24   *Answer*: B.

Explanation: the passage states that fire authorities are responsible for the supervision and enforcement of the regulations. It also says that they may prosecute but the passage does not comment on the authorities' attitude to prosecution so we cannot know if A is correct in its claim that they only do so as a last resort.

Q25   *Answer*: A.

Explanation: the passage only states that local fire authorities are responsible for the supervision and enforcement of the regulations, and supervision means management (enforcement means making happen).

Q26   *Answer*: C.

Explanation: there is insufficient information to tell whether a fire certificate is required in the cases described in suggested answers A, B and D. This is because if no one slept above the first floor or below ground level, then the hotel would not require a certificate. Also the office would only require a fire certificate if more than 20 people worked there. It is clear, however, that a certificate is required by a hotel with accommodation for six people.

Q27 *Answer*: D.

Explanation: the passage states that more than 20 people must work (at any one time) for a certificate to be required. So it is possible that the railway station might not require a fire certificate if not all 20 people worked there at any one time.

Q28 *Answer*: B.

Explanation: the passage states that any site at which explosive or highly flammable material is stored must also obtain a fire certificate.

Q29 *Answer*: C.

Explanation: the passage states that if more than 20 people work at a location at the same time then a certificate is required. With 30 staff the shop probably needs a certificate, but as we do not know how many work there at any one time, it might not require one.

Q30 *Answer*: A.

Explanation: the passage states that as well as complying with the fire regulations some premises also require a fire certificate. This implies that any employer who has a fire certificate must also comply with the fire regulations.

Practice test 2: *using numbers and time*

Q1 *Answer*: 11.21.

Q2 *Answer*: 01.24.

Q3 *Answer*: 03.34.

Q4 *Answer*: 10.16.

Q5 *Answer*: 05.30.

Q6 *Answer*: 77 minutes.

Explanation: 1 hour 17 minutes = 60 + 17 = 77 minutes.

Q7 *Answer*: 6.

Explanation: 24 divided by 4 = 6.

Q8   *Answer*: 03.33.

Explanation: you have to subtract 50 from 04.23. Starting with the minutes 50 – 23 brings us to 4.00 and leaves 27 minutes. 60 – 27 = 33, so the response began at 03.33.

Q9   *Answer*: 700.

Explanation: 2,100 divided by 3 = 700.

Q10   *Answer*: 32 minutes.

Explanation: 09.41 is 19 minutes before 10.00 so 19 + 13 (the time now is 10.13) = 32 minutes.

Q11   *Answer*: 39.

Explanation: 320 – 281 = 39.

Q12   *Answer*: 28 minutes.

Q13   *Answer*: 6.

Explanation: 30 divided by 5 = 6.

Q14   *Answer*: 14.29.

Q15   *Answer*: 27.

Explanation: 9 × 3 = 27.

Q16   *Answer*: 01.38.

Q17   *Answer*: 80.

Explanation: (200 divided by 5) × 2 = 80.

Q18   *Answer*: 200.

Explanation: 3 × 60 = 180 + 20 = 200.

Q19   *Answer*: 310.

Explanation: 297 + 13 = 310.

Q20   *Answer*: 46 minutes.

Q21   *Answer*: 70.

Explanation: 280 divided by 4 = 70.

Q22   *Answer*: 12.05.

Explanation: you have to subtract 70 from 01.15. Subtracting 15 brings us to 01.00 and leaves 55 minutes still to subtract. 60 – 55 = 05, so the response began at 12.05.

Q23   *Answer*: 36 km.

Explanation: 2 × 3 × 6 = 36.

Q24   *Answer*: 52 minutes.

Q25   *Answer*: 44 hours.

Explanation: 100 – 12 = 88. 50 × 88/100 = 44.

Practice test 3: *listening to information*

Passage 1

Q1 *Answer*: False.
   Explanation: the passage states that Southfield is in Newbury.

Q2 *Answer*: False.
   Explanation: the appliance is to visit on Sunday.

Q3 *Answer*: True.
   Explanation: the passage states that 543 are injured each year.

Q4 *Answer*: Cannot say.
   Explanation: the passage states only that the police will be visiting local traders to discourage them from selling fireworks to anyone under the age of 18. From this it cannot be inferred that the traders have actually been doing so.

Q5 *Answer*: False.
   Explanation: the passage states that officers and firefighters are very concerned that someone could end up hurt, from which it can be inferred that no one has been hurt yet.

Passage 2

Q6 *Answer*: Cannot say.
   Explanation: the passage does not say whether the smoke alarms are free.

Q7 *Answer*: True.
   Explanation: the passage states that fire stations will be open to the public, offering advice on fire and community safety.

Q8 *Answer*: False.
   Explanation: the passage states that the batteries last 10 years.

Q9 *Answer*: Cannot say.
   Explanation: the passage states that wherever possible they will be made fully accessible to people with disabilities but it does not say whether or not it will be possible to make them all accessible.

Q10 *Answer*: False.
Explanation: the passage states that over 13,000 have been fitted.

Passage 3

Q11 *Answer*: True.
Explanation: the passage states that over half of the accidental fire deaths in the home were caused by smoking or matches.

Q12 *Answer*: False.
Explanation: the number of boroughs was three.

Q13 *Answer*: Cannot say.
Explanation: the passage states that men were more likely than women to be victims of such an accident and that a higher proportion of deaths occurred in winter. But you cannot infer from this that more men die in the winter months.

Q14 *Answer*: True.

Q15 *Answer*: True.

Passage 4

Q16 *Answer*: False.
Explanation: the passage states that the competition is held every two years.

Q17 *Answer*: True.

Q18 *Answer*: Cannot say.
Explanation: the accident involves two cars but the number of dummies is not stated.

Q19 *Answer*: True.

Q20 *Answer*: False.
Explanation: the passage states that the competition involves teams of firefighters from all over the country, so it is not international.

Passage 5

Q21 *Answer*: True.

Explanation: the passage states that people must realize that they are doing something really quite dangerous.

Q22 *Answer*: Cannot say.

Explanation: the passage states that this is the cause of the most common fire in the kitchen but does not say what the most common sort of fire is in general.

Q23 *Answer*: True.

Explanation: the passage states that water on the food could cause the oil to explode.

Q24 *Answer*: True.

Q25 *Answer*: True.

Explanation: the passage states that the pan should not be more than a third full, which is the same as 33.3 per cent.

Passage 6

Q26 *Answer*: False.

Explanation: the passage states that it took three hours, not over three hours.

Q27 *Answer*: True.

Q28 *Answer*: False.

Explanation: the passage states that the exercise was held in Bank Station.

Q29 *Answer*: Cannot say.

Explanation: the passage makes no mention of this issue.

Q30 *Answer*: True.

Explanation: the commissioner's comments support this statement.

Passage 7

Q31 *Answer*: False.
Explanation: the passage states that the strategy is for England and Wales.

Q32 *Answer*: True.
Explanation: the passage states that they must develop a broader role.

Q33 *Answer*: False.
Explanation: it was described as a White Paper.

Q34 *Answer*: Cannot say.
Explanation: the reasons for the changes are not mentioned in the passage.

Q35 *Answer*: True.

Passage 8

Q36 *Answer*: True.
Explanation: the passage states that the largest single cause of deaths and injuries from fire is accidental fires in the home.

Q37 *Answer*: True.
Explanation: the passage states that there is a growing trend in deliberate fires.

Q38 *Answer*: Cannot say.
Explanation: the passage states that the poorest in our society are most at risk from deliberately started fires but does not say that they are more likely to start these fires.

Q39 *Answer*: False.
Explanation: the passage describes other important roles of the service.

Q40 *Answer*: Cannot say.
Explanation: the passage makes no comment on this issue.

With over 42 years of publishing, more than 80 million people have succeeded in business with thanks to **Kogan Page**

www.koganpage.com